Edgar Morin has been urging for a shift t
unique capability to move between the n;
any injustice—and is ideally placed to ad
of our times. What makes Morin uniqu
turns a critical eye on complexity theory itself, resisting a return to determinism, ...
disjunction in come approaches to complexity.

In this extremely valuable volume of translated essays he turns his attention to the technical and philosophical underpinnings of complexity theory and applies it to a wide-ranging number of issues including the nature of scientific thinking, self-organisation, action theory, the notion of the subject, education, the idea of solidarity and the idea of the "enterprise." These essays will certainly stimulate the critical debate within complexity circles, but is also essential reading for anybody interested in our complex world and how to live in it.

Paul Cilliers, University of Stellenbosch—Author of *Complexity and Postmodernism*

Here is a discussion that takes us into the puzzling domain of self in relation to eco-organization. We normally relate the notion of complexity to technical order, which has led, in Morin's phrase, to "blind intelligence." He postulates a domain of complexity in which living order has a crucial organizing role. By providing a satisfying explanation of the processes of recursion and a perspective of holism in which activities of the whole, "emergents," loop back to constrain parts, Morin's valuable presentation reveals how environment is in us.

Peter J. C. Harries-Jones, PhD—Emeritus Professor, York University,
Author of a *Recursive Vision: Ecological Understanding and Gregory Bateson*

Morin has opened the way to real thinking about human nature, not reducing it to one of its components, bio-physico-chemical, social, psychological, religious, or political. Understanding the interactions between these components without confusion is the challenge of the sciences of complexity.

Henri Atlan—Author, *Enlightenment to Enlightenment: Intercritique of Science and Myth*,
Hadassah University Hospital, Jerusalem, Israel, EHESS, Paris

The biology of 21st century is moving from the reductionist approach of molecular biology to the systems approach of the new science of systems biology. More than 20 years ago Edgar Morin had already articulated the paradigm of complexity that gives us the clues needed to address the conceptual changes in modern biology.

Magali Roux-Rouquié—Senior scientist-CNRS (French National Research Center),
Deputy director USAR-CNRS

Morin is a representative thinker of humanity's planetary age. In remedying the deficiency of Western classic analytic thinking, Morin's complex thinking shows some affinities to the Chinese classic synthetic thinking, such as the emphasis on the union of the universal and the particular. Morin's path indicates that the creation of the paradigm of complexity depends on the fusion of Western and Eastern thinking, each of which has its strength and weakness.

Yi-zhuang Chen—Professor of Philosophy, Central-South University, People's Republic
of China

The Apollo of complexity, Edgar Morin is a solar presence, helping us to live and to hope. His work constitutes a major contribution to transdisciplinarity.

Basarab Nicolescu—Theoretical physicist, CNRS, University of Paris 6, Professor,
University Babes-Bolyai de Cluj, Rumania, President, CIRET (International Center
for Research on Transdisciplinary, Studies) Author of *Manifesto of Transdisciplinarity*

Morin's reflections on complexity can be profitably mined for nuggets of insights by complexity scientists and interdisciplinarians alike.

William H. Newell—Miami University, Executive Director, Association for Integrative
Studies

I have not been this excited about anything rooted in general system theory since reading von Bertalanffy and Boulding many years ago. As one invested in interpretive epistemology and related methodologies, I had all but given up any hope of inspiration from this quarter. But Edgar Morin has changed all that with this marvelous book. Not only does he reinvigorate general systems theory, and its close companion complexity theory, by giving their epistemological foundations some much needed attention, he has laid down a tantalizing challenge to think more complexly about everything from self to society and provided plenty of inspiration for doing so. I hope that all my colleagues in organization studies will read this book and respond to it. It is deserving not only of our attention, but will be of interest to those working in all the fields of science, social science and the humanities.

Mary Jo Hatch—Author, *Organization Theory: Modern, Symbolic, and Postmodern Perspectives*, Professor Emeritus, McIntire School of Commerce, University of Virginia, USA

It is apt that Edgar Morin's book should be published at the beginning at the new Millennium because what he is proposing is a radical shift in the scientific paradigm. In place of separate sciences, all based upon a static, closed, regulated and law-abiding universe, Morin offers a trans-scientific view of the messy reality of hazard, uncertainty, accident and confusion. In this he suggests a creative, dynamic view of the world. At home in the newer disciplines of complexity theory, cybernetics and systems theories, he goes beyond them to represent a well based view of a vital world of novelty and life. The life sciences of biology, evolution, sociology, and business organization all would benefit from this refreshing and novel approach that looks at the world as we encounter it, not as it is filtered through the lenses of specialized, and isolated scientific disciplines.

Albert Low—Author of *Creating Consciousness*, Teacher, Montreal Zen Center

Italy ranks among the countries that have paid closest attention to Morin's evocative reflections on complexity. Morin's work has had a profound impact on the nation's scientific, educational, and political landscape.

Sergio Manghi—Professor of Sociology, University of Parma

Edgar Morin's writing on film, its stars, and the human beings who engage with them, remains the richest treatment of these phenomena available. Magic, wonder, the poetic as well as the prosaic, are a feature of his work generally, which refuses reductiveness while maintaining rigor. An intellectual monument in France, his theory and commentary—passionate, ethically engaged and never leaving the life out of life—is at last beginning to have the impact it deserves in the English-speaking world.

Lorraine Mortimer—Senior Lecturer in Sociology and Anthropology, La Trobe University, Melbourne

Someone once said that the avoidance of complexity is the essence of tyranny. For this reason alone, Edgar Morin's book is worth reading. Even more, we need to embrace and to understand complexity.

Ian Mitroff—Professor Emeritus, University of Southern California, University Professor, Alliant International University, Visiting Professor, UC Berkeley

What I like best in the work of Edgar Morin is the fundamental difference he makes between what is complex and what is just complicated. The real world is complex, meaning that antagonism and complementarity go hand in hand. Once I understood this, and other aspects of Morin's paradigm of complexity, my research took a new turn.

Peter Westbroek—Professor of Geophysiology, University of Leiden, The Netherlands

ON COMPLEXITY

ADVANCES IN SYSTEMS THEORY, COMPLEXITY, AND THE HUMAN SCIENCES
Alfonso Montuori, Series Editor

Mind and Nature: A Necessary Unity
Gregory Bateson

Angels Fear
Gregory Bateson & Mary Catherine Bateson

Our Own Metaphor
Mary Catherine Bateson

The Narrative Universe
Gianluca Bocchi & Mauro Ceruti

Evolution Without Foundations
Mauro Ceruti

Mind in Time: The Dynamics of Thought, Reality, and Consciousness
Allan Combs, Mark Germine, & Ben Goertzel (eds.)

Politics, Persuasion and Polity: A Theory of Democratic Self-Organization
Gus di Zerega

Evolution: The Grand Synthesis
Ervin Laszlo

The Systems View of the World
Ervin Laszlo

On Complexity
Edgar Morin

Homeland Earth: A Manifesto for the New Millennium
Edgar Morin & Anne Brigitte Kern

A Tripartite Seed
Gordon Rowland

New Paradigms, Culture and Subjectivity
Dora Fried Schnitman (ed.)

ON COMPLEXITY

Edgar Morin

Translated by Robin Postel

HAMPTON PRESS, INC.
CRESSKILL, NEW JERSEY

Printed in the United States of America

Library of Congress Cataloging-in-Publication Data

Morin, Edgar.
  [Complexité humaine. English]
  On complexity / Edgar Morin.
    p. cm. -- (Advances in systems theory, complexity, and the human sciences)
  Includes bibliographical references and index.
  ISBN 978-1-57273-801-0 (paperbound)
1. Complexity (Philosophy) I. Title.
  B105.C473M67513 2008
  117--dc22

                        2008002108

Translated from the French by Robin Postel, except Chapters 6-7 and Appendix 1 which have been translated by Sean M. Kelly.

Hampton Press, Inc.
23 Broadway
Cresskill, NJ 07626

http://hamptonpress.com/

CONTENTS

FOREWORD
EDGAR MORIN'S PATH
OF COMPLEXITY

Alfonso Montuori

The reform in thinking is a key anthropological and historical problem. This implies a mental revolution of considerably greater proportions than the Copernican revolution. Never before in the history of humanity have the responsibilities of thinking weighed so crushingly on us.

Edgar Morin

Does knowing that knowledge cannot be guaranteed by a foundation not mean that we have already acquired a first fundamental knowledge? And should this not lead us to abandon the architectural metaphor, in which the term "foundation" assumes an indispensable meaning, in favor of a musical metaphor of construction in movement that transforms in its very movement the constitutive elements that form it? And might we not also consider the knowledge of knowledge as a construction in movement?

Edgar Morin

We need a kind of thinking that reconnects that which is disjointed and compartmentalized, that respects diversity as it recognizes unity, and that tries to discern interdependencies. We need a radical thinking (which gets to the root of problems), a multidimensional thinking, and an organizational or systemic thinking.

Edgar Morin

History has not reached a stagnant end, nor is it triumphantly marching towards the radiant future. It is being catapulted into an unknown adventure.

Edgar Morin

EDGAR MORIN: A BIBLIO–BIOGRAPHY

Perhaps the best way to provide a contextual introduction to Morin's work is through an outline of his intellectual trajectory, in the form of a "biblio-biography." A review of Morin's journey helps us, I believe, to better understand the man and his mission in the essays that follow.

Edgar Morin's work has been tremendously influential in Europe, Latin America, and French-speaking Africa. Numerous monographs discussing his work have been written in France, Spain, Italy, Brazil, Canada, and England (Anselmo, 2005, 2006; Bianchi, 2001; Fages, 1980; Fortin, 2002; Kofman, 1996; Rosetto Ajello, 2003). The extent of his influence in diverse and even remote fields exceeds perhaps even Gregory Bateson's. Emeritus Director of Research at the CNRS (the French National Research Center), Morin has received honorary doctorates (appropriately in subjects ranging from political science to psychology to sociology) from universities including Messina, Geneva, Milan, La Paz, Odense, Perugia, Cosenza, Palermo, Nuevo Leon (Mexico), Brussels, Valencia, the Catholic University of Porto Alegre, and the Universidade Federal do Rio Grande do Norte, among others, and holds an itinerant UNESCO chair in Complex Thought. Morin's imprint is to be found in fields ranging from media studies to visual anthropology to cinema verité to philosophy to action research to sociology to systems theory to ecology to education, and recently with increasing frequency in the hard sciences. Just to give a small indication of the range of his influence, in English, a language in which his work is relatively little known, he is cited by such diverse scholars as historian of religion Mircea Eliade (Eliade, 1978), sociologist Lewis Coser (Coser, 1997), psychoanalyst Andre Green (Green, 2005), physicist Basarab Nicolescu (Nicolescu, 1997), philosopher Julia Kristeva (Kristeva, 1997), historian Daniel J. Boorstin (Boorstin, 1992), philosophers of science Gianluca Bocchi and Mauro Ceruti (Bocchi & Ceruti, 2002), Islamic scholar and Moroccan Imam Abdessalam Yassine (Yassine, 2000), mathematician William Byers (Byers, 2007), Mexican Nobel Laureate in Literature Octavio Paz (Paz, 1986), Iain Chambers, the English scholar of cultural and postcolonial studies (Chambers, 1994), and therapist/philosopher Paul Watzlawick (Watzlawick, 1977).

As Kofman states in his volume on Morin for the Pluto Press series on *Modern European Thinkers,*

> Morin's approach is in harmony with a new culture of uncertainty as instanced in the literary and philosophic writings of Derrida, Levinas, or Deleuze. But unlike his fellow travelers Morin has been alone in daring to attempt a method which connects sciences and philosophy through complexity. In French intellectual life today Morin is a now leader but still an outsider. (Kofman, 1996)

The 21st century has seen several research centers devoted to Morin's work, including one at the University of Messina in Sicily, and most notably the inauguration of *Multiversidad Mundo Real Edgar Morin*, a university in Hermosillo (Sonora) Mexico, based on the principles of Morin's work.

Morin's books address such a variety of issues that it's necessary to first catalog some of them, at least a small selection out of the 60 or so books he has published, in order to get an idea of the scope of his work. In the process, we can begin to see the "path laid down in walking," and to recognize the threads that tie much of Morin's work together.

For a useful introduction to Morin in English, the reader is referred to Myron Kofman's (1996) *Edgar Morin: From Big Brother to Fraternity*, in the Pluto Press Modern European Thinkers series. Kofman is particularly good on the historical context and Morin's experience with Hegelian-Marxism. Given the relatively short space here, and the vast range of Morin's experience, I refer to Kofman's work for a discussion of this fascinating period and its influence on Morin's thought. Morin's *Homeland Earth* offers an accessible introduction to his socio-political and moral thought.

Beginnings . . .

Morin's first book was *L'An Zero de l'Allemagne* [Germany Year Zero], written right after the end of World War II when Morin, then in his mid-20s, was in Germany with the French Army. *Germany Year Zero* was his effort to document the devastation of one of Europe's most sophisticated and cultured countries, the home of Goethe, Beethoven, Kant, and other towering figures of western civilization. It was an attempt to understand how such a country could have been overtaken by the horror of the Nazi era. Central to the book is Morin's unwillingness to reduce Germany and Germans to "sale boches" (filthy Germans), and to assess the horror of the situation in a broad context and with an unusual depth of feeling. Here we already find a cornerstone of what Morin, the Jewish resistance fighter who lived in mortal danger during the war years, would later called *complex thought*, his refusal to reduce and thereby mutilate. Briefly, complex thought does not reduce and polarize. Morin does not want to reduce Germany and its people to the actions of the Nazis, which in the immediate aftermath of the war was all too easily done. This refusal to reduce, to take a Manichean, simplistic view (a view that is often driven by fear, anger, and other emotions, but often masquerades as coldly rational), is a central element of Morin's thought.

The term *reductionism* is used with great, perhaps excessive, frequency these days. With Morin it is not some theoretical abstraction, a form of namecalling. Instead, with Morin it emerges from, and is embedded in, the existential reality of daily life. It manifests in the unwillingness to take a reductionist stance to the German people. It refuses to equate Germans and Germany only with the Nazis and the Holocaust. It would be all too easy to say that the German reduction of Jews warrants an equal reduction of Germans, as "pure evil," or some similar stance. But Morin insists on viewing Germans in their full complexity. He explores why and how, given the complexity of the German people, they fell victim to the Nazi scourge. And most importantly, he always reminds us that as human beings we are *all* vulnerable to episodes of madness. Morin reminds us that the dualism of good versus evil all too easily leads us to believe that "they" are "evil," and "we" are by definition "good," and therefore anything we do is also by definition good and legitimate. Crucial here is that the belief in "our" inherent goodness is accompanied by a lack of self-reflection and self-criticism, usually with disastrous results. The participation of the observer in every observation, the role of self-reflection and self-inquiry in inquiry, the dangers of reduction and disjunction, and the often hidden motives of the quest for certainty will be central and recurring themes in all of Morin's work. As Selvini Palazzoli (1990) writes:

> Since, in the relationship between observing and observed system, the observer is as much part of the observed system as the observed system is part of the intellect and culture of the observing system, Morin finds that the observer observes himself while he observes the system. (p. 128)

Another theme from Morin's earliest works that later came up in a debate in 2000 with Jacques Derrida in the pages of *Le Monde* is Morin's insistence on the vital importance of forgiveness. For Derrida, forgiveness should be an exception, at the edge of impossibility. For Morin, forgiveness is a resistance to the cruelty of the world—the title of his response to Derrida (Morin, February 2000). Once again, this involves precisely the refusal to perpetuate the very attitudes that provoke conflict and keep the cycle of violence and hatred going. Forgiveness is what takes us beyond simplistic, dualistic thinking, and leads us toward a *politics of civilization* (Morin & Nair, 1997). For Morin, forgiveness is a virtue we must cultivate, even when it seems easier and more immediate to hate.

It should be pointed out that Morin's work is by no means saccharine or Pollyanna-ish, devoid of realism and ungrounded in an awareness of the real terror humans have inflicted upon each other. Indeed, in his popular book *Homeland Earth* (Morin & Kern, 1999), he speaks of a "Gospel of Doom" that recognizes our fate and invites us to stare it in the face and view it as an invitation for human solidarity, to come together under the recognition that we are all in the same existential boat. In Morin we find a mature compassion that comes from having experienced first-hand, as a resistance fighter and French citizen, the horror that was unleashed on his own country and the rest of Europe. Morin's unwillingness to demonize might be viewed as a "tender-minded" unwillingness to face the harsh realities of life and take a stand, a position of "friendly weakness." Nothing could be further from the truth. In fact, Morin's view is that the cycle of horror and violence will be perpetuated precisely because we demonize others and are unwilling to forgive, to recognize the extent to which we all, as humans, are capable of an extreme range of behaviors. The unquestioned belief in one's own "goodness" can lead, through a process Jung called "enantiodromia," to a coincidence of opposites, where the very actions taken to fight the enemy bring about the conditions that the enemy's victory would ensure. Where, for instance, a democratic country fighting a totalitarian regime resorts to such drastic draconian actions that it actually destroys the very democratic principles it is allegedly attempting to safeguard.

Morin has a strong affinity for certain aspects of Buddhism, having seen the extent of our human capacity for love and hate, our intelligence and our stupidity. His wisdom and compassion come from having looked within and without deeply and with great depth of feeling. As the eminent sociologist Alain Touraine wrote, quoting the African Terentius, it can be said of Morin, more than any thinker in our era, that nothing human is alien to him (Touraine, 2001). This includes, for instance, recognizing that the gruesome actions of ordinary German citizens were not performed by exceptional, evil monsters, but by ordinary human beings. Research in social psychology, from Milgram to Zimbardo, was later to show how "the power of the situation" could turn educated citizens into Nazi killers. "Nice" Stanford students could, within a matter of hours, treat "prisoners" in an experimental setting, their fellow students, much the same way that some military personnel in tremendously stressful and exceptional conditions treated prisoners whom they believed would not think twice about killing them if released. Morin's particular gift is to show us how there, but for the grace of God, go all of us.

Morin's first book was the inspiration for the classic Italian neo-Realist movie *Germany Year Zero* [Germania Anno Zero] by Roberto Rossellini. Morin has had an ongoing relationship of mutual influence with the arts and artists around the world. This is another aspect of his work that makes him so unique in the often dreary and secluded world of the social sciences. Examples include Morin's delightful reflections about *New York*, a collaboration with Dutch visual artist Karel Appel (Morin & Appel, 1984), and his influence on, among others, the great Brazilian songwriter Caetano Veloso, who explicitly discusses the importance of Morin's work for his artistic vision and for Brazil's resistance against authoritarian government (Veloso, 2003), and his relationship with such figures as novelist Marguerite Duras. Most recently we have seen the publication of *Peuples*, a book of photographs of peoples from all over the world by Pierre de Vallombreuse with Morin's commentary (de Vallombreuse & Morin, 2006).

Morin's next work was *L'Homme et la Mort* [Humanity and Death] (1951). Here we find, in typically Morinian fashion, a sustained meditation on death that is both deeply personal and planetary, both *holographic* and *multidimensional*, to use terms Morin was to employ later. It is personal, because Morin lost his mother at an early age, and the event affected him profoundly. It haunts his work in too many ways to address in this brief sketch. A thoughtful discussion of the role Morin's mother's death played in his life can be found in Heinz Weinmann's introduction to the collection of Morin essays entitled *La Complexitè Humaine* (Morin, 1994b). Morin's work is planetary in scope because he explores death cross-culturally in the great religions and spiritual traditions, throughout human history, and in the sciences, finding that the plurality of interpretive frameworks shed light, each in a different way, on the most profound event. Morin's work has always had this holographic, multidimensional quality: the part and the whole are always interconnected, and one finds the part in the whole and the whole in the part; and the subject is approached from a variety of dimensions, from the biological to the cultural to the psychological and mythological.

Morin's approach has always been both planetary and personal. We later find wonderful examples of this holographic method in *Vidal et les Siens* [Vidal and his People] (Morin, 1996), which is at once a biography of his father, Vidal, a history of Sephardic Jews, and a history of Europe, and in *Pour Sortir du Ventieme Siecle* [Entering the 20th Century] (Morin, 2004b), in which Morin addresses key political issues through a combination of theoretical and historical reflection on the state of the world grounded with examples from his own experience.

Morin's book on death brings together two themes that will recur throughout his work. The motivation for inquiry emerges from personal experience, most dramatically with the death of his mother, not abstract speculation or disciplinary agendas. Another key element in this work is transdisciplinarity. Morin's inquiry is not limited to one discipline. It draws on a whole range of *pertinent knowledge* (Morin, 2001b). In other words, he is not approaching his subject from what I have elsewhere called a *discipline-driven* perspective (Montuori, 2005). He is not driven by problem solving in the context of the agenda of a specific discipline. Rather, he is motivated by his own experience, in this case his loss, by the need to make sense of lived human experience, his own and that of every other human being. This is central to what makes Morin's vision of transdisciplinarity so important and so timely: it is grounded not in attempts to create abstract theoretical frameworks, or to further the agenda of a new discipline, but in the need to find knowledge that is pertinent for the human quest to understand and make sense of lived experience, and of the "big questions," which are usually left out of academic discourse precisely because they are too complex and transdisciplinary. Lived experience simply cannot satisfactorily be reduced to the perspective of one discipline.

Autocritique

Morin's early work on death shows his willingness to grapple with profound existential issues so often obliterated in the all-too-often sterile discourse of social science and philosophy. This existential aliveness, this grounding in the lived experience of the realities of existence, is present in Morin's work whether he is discussing cybernetics, cinema, self-organization, ecology, politics, or education. Morin's work does not come from an attempt to escape life for an ivory tower, or to control it through intricate theoretical frameworks and maps, but from an effort to immerse himself in it more deeply, and to provide the sciences with tools to account more adequately for the lived complexity of life, and indeed to assist the reader in that process of immersion. Morin characterizes his later work on complex thought as an attempt to develop a method that does not "mutilate," that does not fragment and abstract, that does not do violence to life, by giving is a unidimensional, anemic, antiseptic, homogenized *pars pro toto*. This transdisciplinary approach could later be seen in the journal *Arguments* that Morin led along with Roland Barthes, Kostas Axelos, and others from 1956 to 1962. The broad range of topics addressed in the journal reflected a focus on issues rather than disciplinary agendas, and a willingness to range far and wide.

After World War II, the influence of the Left and of the communist party in European thought was enormous. There were very clear boundaries with which to assess what was considered to be outside the party line. Morin's independent thought was clearly transgressive, and in *Autocritique* Morin (2004a) documents his expulsion from the party for writing an "inappropriate" article. Morin's *Autocritique* is a remarkable document from an "engaged" intellectual grappling with the complexities of politics and self-deception. It is a model of honesty and self-reflection and provides us with rare visibility into the life and thought of a man in the thick of the events that were shaping European and indeed planetary culture at that time, primarily Stalin's rise to power and the repression in the Eastern block countries. Drake (2002) provides some context. He writes that Morin was "one of the few PCF (French Communist Party) intellectuals who refused to blindly follow the Party line" (p. 70). Exploring such phenomena as self-deception, cognitive dissonance, groupthink, and authoritarian/totalitarian thinking and behavior in himself and in "the party," we find another theme that will run through all of Morin's future work. In his 7 *Complex Lessons in Education for the Future* (Morin, 2001b), a document Morin wrote at the request of UNESCO, the first lesson is about self-deception and combating "error and illusion." How is it that we let ourselves literally become possessed by ideas, by the party, by our "faith," by our "cause," even by what we believe to be "science?"

The fierce independence of judgment so characteristic of creative individuals (Barron, 1995) has always marked Morin's life and work. It has often made him unpopular with those who would find shelter in the warm embrace of "in-group" conformity, those who want to tow the ideological line and build strong immune defenses around the hard nucleus of doctrine—the core that cannot be challenged (Morin, 1991). Morin never "belonged" in the sense of relinquishing his own independence to gain the considerable favors offered by those who were "connected" and "insiders," whether in the form of publishing contracts, intellectual movements, or, ironically, notoriety in the United States. Whereas there are some parallels between Morin's thought and some of the French authors associated in the United States with the postmodern turn (and, it should be noted, some pointed and vital differences), Morin has never associated himself with postmodernism as a movement and intellectual bandwagon and rarely if ever uses the term. French authors who are closely associated with postmodernism were extensively published in the United States, while authors who were considered major figures in France were sidelined because they could not be identified with the hot new trend. It is interesting to note that in the United States French thought over the last few decades is associated almost exclusively with postmodernism. In France, on the other hand, postmodernism is considered a largely Anglophone phenomenon (Journet, 2000).

In non-English speaking countries, ranging from Brazil to Colombia to Italy and Spain, and in France itself, of course, Morin has been recognized as one of the most significant thinkers of our time. The gap between the Anglophone world and the rest of the planet is fascinating, and speaks volumes about the inevitably partial nature of any understanding of European intellectual life determined as it is by publishers, mastery of languages other than English (since translations are themselves a whole other issues, as evidenced by the highly problematic English translations of Piaget, for instance), and other issues.

Autocritique (Morin, 2004a) marks an important turning point for Morin. We normally assume that we have ideas; however, it became clear to Morin that ideas can also have us—literally possess us. Human beings can literally be possessed by ideologies and belief systems, whether on the left or the right, whether in science or religion. Henceforth, Morin's effort will be to develop a form of thinking—and of being in the world—that is always self-reflective and self-critical, always open and creative, always eager to challenge the fundamental assumptions underlying a system of thought, and always alert for the ways in which, covertly or overtly, we create inviolate centers that cannot be questioned or challenged. Knowledge always requires the knowledge of knowledge, the ongoing investigation and interrogation of how we construct knowledge. Indeed, *Knowledge of Knowledge* is the title of the third volume of Morin's *Method* (Morin, 1986).

Sociology and Popular Culture

At the same time that Morin was exploring such a weighty subject as death and engaging in a very public political "self-critique" of his participation in the Communist party, and the way that this applied holographically to the larger issues of the role of ideologies and totalitarianism and participation in larger planetary culture, he was also beginning to write a series of books on what might be initially thought of as "lighter fare." In the mid to late 1950s and early 1960s, Morin wrote path-breaking works about cinema, the star system, and popular culture. Several of these books, originally published from the mid 1950s to the early 1960s, have been published or re-issued in the United States by the University of Minnesota Press (Morin, 2005a, 2005b). Morin's innovative work in this area has been recognized as crucially important—both prescient and still vitally relevant in a discussion that has often drowned in vapid and sensationalist scholarship. As Lorraine Mortimer writes in the introduction to *Cinema, or the Imaginary Man* (Morin, 2005b), Morin's book was a breath of fresh air in 1959, when much of the discourse on cinema was highly critical of bourgeois entertainment, viewing it as opium for the masses that promoted capitalist values. Mortimer pointedly reminds us of how the sociologist Pierre Bourdieu attacked Morin's study of mass culture because it was "an instrument of alienation at the service of capitalism to divert the proletariat from its revolutionary mission" (Mortimer, 2001, p. 78). This once again gives us an idea of Morin's constant battle against reductionism, the attempt to reduce a complex phenomenon to one potential aspect and manifestation, and in the process dismiss it.

In the case of Bourdieu, we find a view of cinema that does not take into account the infinite emotional, social, and other complexities that the experience affords us. It is deeply doctrinaire by reducing the enormous complexity of cinema to, in Bourdieu's trite and cliché–ridden critique, "an instrument of alienation at the service of capitalism to divert the proletariat from its revolutionary mission." In the late 1950s in *The Stars* (Morin, 2005a), he was also the only thinker associated with the at the time completely counter-cultural idea that the cult of celebrity has a strong religious component (Young, 2002). Interestingly, Young goes on to cite research conducted in the United Kingdom and the United States that suggests celebrity worship does indeed play a role similar to that of religion and is the source of new "myths" and mythical figures in today's society.

Morin was one of the first academics to take popular culture seriously. His psychoanalytically influenced discussion of interiority, subjectivity, dreams, myth, his use of the concepts of projection and introjection, and his focus on creativity and the imagination acknowledged the importance of understanding popular cultural phenomena that clearly had, and continue to have, an enormous impact on people's lives. Among other things, Morin studied the seemingly trivial fan letters written to movie stars in popular magazines, identifying the mechanisms of projection and identification in the adulation of "stars." Again we see Morin moving from the macro role of popular culture to the micro, the specific examples of individual gestures of fans toward their idols. This reflects a guiding principle of Morin's work, found in Pascal's statement that it is impossible to understand the whole without understanding the part, and impossible to understand the part without understanding the whole. In *Method*, Morin would later use this as an entry point to critique both reductionism and holism.

But why this sudden detour into cinema? Morin's research is motivated by his own life experiences. After the death of his mother, the young Morin became an obsessive movie-goer, and developed a fascination for the magical dimensions of cinema. It allowed him to temporarily inhabit and dream of a different world, escape his pain, and immerse himself in a world of creativity and imagination through a ritualistic process not unlike the experiences of art of our distant ancestors, glimpses of art illuminated by flickering lights in dark caves. It is a commonplace to say that one's research is really a reflection of one's life. But in Morin's case this is particularly evident, and central, as I have suggested, to his transdisciplinary approach, which does not seek to simply solve a problem, but is a quest for meaning derived from his own personal experience, and clearly from that of millions of other movie-goers.

In 1961, film-maker Jean Rouch and Edgar Morin made the documentary *Chronicle of a Summer*. Set in Paris in the aftermath of the Algerian war and before the explosion of riots that played such a role in the 1960s, culminating in the events of 1968, this documentary holds the distinction of being recognized as the first example of *cinéma verité*. It breaks down the barrier between the camera and the subject in a precursor to a far more participative approach to inquiry and documenting events, and the more recent excesses of "reality television." Roland Barthes wrote, "What this film engages is humanity itself." In his review of documentary filmmaking, *Claiming the Real: The Documentary Film Revisited*, Brian Winston (1995) referred to *Chronicle of a Summer* as the key cinema verité film.

The documentary had a profound influence on French film-maker Jean-Luc Godard, and has become a classic of documentary making and visual anthropology. Particularly important is the self-reflective dimension, which includes interviewees being filmed observing footage of their interviews, creating a self-reflective loop (Ungar, 2003). This innovative approach shows Morin's lifelong concern for inter-subjectivity and self-reflection that was later to be articulated extensively in his works of sociology and complex thought (Morin, 1994b, 1994c, 2008).

The publication of *Introduction à une politique de l'homme. Arguments politiques* [Introduction to a politics of humanity. Political perspectives] (Morin, 1999a) in 1965 was the next step in Morin's political reflections. Here Morin explored the nature of human nature in the political context, critiquing Marx, Freud, and other currents of thought, including a trenchant critique of the notion of "development," while developing his notion of a planetary politics and planetary culture, which he was to elaborate in later works. Essential here was Morin's excavation of the underlying assumptions of the various approaches to understanding and framing human nature, which he was to return to in the work that became the predecessor to his magnum opus, *Method, Le Paradigme Perdu* [Paradigm Lost] (Morin, 1979). Morin's transdisciplinary approach crosses and integrates a plurality of disciplines, and a key dimension of transdisciplinarity is understanding the way that knowledge is constructed in various disciplines and approaches (Montuori, 2005a). Morin's work is radical in this sense because it traces the roots of knowledge, digging deep to find the underlying assumptions that form the foundations for the differing perspectives. Transdisciplinarity explicitly surfaces the assumptions of the many different disciplines it addresses. Although not demanding in-depth expertise and specialization to quite the same extent that a discipline-based researcher might have, transdisciplinary research does demand a more philosophical or meta-paradigmatic position that steps back to observe how different paradigms shape the construction of knowledge, exploring the roots of the disciplines. The point is to become aware of one's own assumptions about the process of inquiry, as well as to uncover the assumptions of the various perspectives that inform inquiry.

Morin's next two works, written in the mid-1960s, followed somewhat naturally from his *Cinéma Verité* documentary. They focused on innovative, participatory approaches to social research, what he called a "sociology of the present," using a "multidimensional method." Both of these works were fortunately translated into English. *The Red and the White* (Morin, 1970), a study of modernization in the Breton village of Plozevet, utilized Morin's "phenomenographic" approach, a precursor to the recent boom in qualitative research methodologies, at a time when most if not all sociological research was quantitative. Morin and his research team actively participated in the life of the village and collected data in a variety of ways, from the quantitative to the qualitative, by living in the village and keeping diaries about their experience as researchers. These diaries and have recently been published in their entirety (Morin, 2001a). *The Red and the White* shows Morin's desire to capture the full complexity and richness of this village, and the realization that traditional sociological methods simply did not come close to this—they did not address the lived experience of human beings undergoing a major social change.

Rumor in Orleans (Morin, 1971) is the fascinating and disturbing account of a rumor about alleged white slave trade conducted by Jews in the city of Orleans, which led to some degree of panic and attacks on stores owned by Jews. Morin's research managed to unravel the web and actually laid the rumor to rest. Again we see Morin at the leading edge of thought with what would be called "action research" today. Morin broke down the assumptions that research should be quantitative and place the researcher as "the expert," "objectively" studying his "subject." His research was also an intervention, and an example of "clinical sociology." For Morin, this research is also a critique of universalism, the search for laws and grand theories, and a valorization of what he called "the event"—the unique, the unrepeatable, the destabilizing moment—and crisis as an opportunity for inquiry, a subject he was later to explore in his work on "crisiology" (Morin, 1993, 1994c).

Discussing his methodology, Morin wrote:

> Our method seeks to envelop the phenomenon (observation), to recognize the forces within it (praxis), to provoke it at strategic points (intervention), to penetrate it by individual contact (interview), to question action, speech, and things.
>
> Each of these methods poses the fundamental methodological problem: the relationship between the research worker and the subject.
>
> It is not merely a subject-object relationship. The "object" of the inquiry is both object and subject, and one cannot escape the intersubjective character of relations between men.
>
> We believe the optimal relationship requires, on the one hand, detachment and objectivity in relation to the object as object, and on the other, participation and sympathy in relation to the object as subject. As this object and subject are one, our approach must be a dual one. (Morin, 1970, p. 259)

From his work on popular culture to *cinéma verité* to his participatory research approach, Morin challenges assumptions about high and low culture, the objectivity and distance of the researcher and the camera, and the critique of expertism that instead favors immersion and participation in the everyday, and draws on the knowledge of nonspecialized participants. This is part of Morin's larger thrust to bring the discourse of social science in much closer relationship to the lived realities of human experience, the contingencies, the seeming trivialities, the emotions, subjectivities, and uniqueness of life in all its manifestations, while at the same time uncovering the epistemological dimension, addressing how we make sense of the world, how we construct our knowledge.

Journals

In the early 1960s Morin began publishing selected journals. These were very personal reflections and explorations that chronicled his experiences from the very mundane to the dramatic, from the profound philosophical and psycho-logical reflections of *Le Vif du Sujet* (Morin, 1982) to the account of his voyage to China in the 1990s (Morin, 1992b). These documents showed the author grappling with issues in the moment, and with his own responses to the crises he was facing, whether intellectual or personal. Particularly fascinating is the *California Journal*, soon to be published in English. This is an account of Morin's year in California during the height of the 1960s, spent at the Salk Institute in San Diego, in the company of Jonas Salk, François Jacob, and Anthony Wilden, among others. Morin immersed himself in biology, cybernetics, and systems theories, and reflected on the dramatic social changes he was witnessing. *California Journal* provides a vibrant portrait of a changing society by a complex man whose Mediterranean sensibility pervades his life and work. Tellingly, we find none of the mixture of condescension and envy found in the now-popular travelogues of European intellectuals in the United States.

Many of his closest colleagues and collaborators have considered Morin's journals to be some of his deepest and most significant contributions. The author's voice, already so vivid in his scholarly works, becomes even more alive in these pages, as we go behind the scenes during the writing of a book, during a television appearance, apartment-hunting in Paris, or at a conference. Ironically, some of Morin's journals have been attacked by critics who have found them lacking the "seriousness" one should find in an academic. Apparently intellectuals can write weighty tomes about popular culture (now that Morin has contributed to making it an acceptable subject of study) but can-not admit to enjoying it. It seems the serious academic is not entitled to discuss that s/he eats and drinks, watches late night television, or enjoys soccer, but only superciliously reflect on the extent to which "the masses" are bamboozled by the media and pop culture—a clear hangover from the attitude that Bourdieu represented so clearly. It's acceptable to look at the impact of popular culture on others, but not on the academic him or herself. Academia is still very suspicious of "subjectivity," which essentially amounts to the everyday experience of life, and particularly of the subjectivity of the academic! One's subjectivity, one's domestic life need to be neatly compartmentalized and strictly separated from one's life as a scholar. Although it is acceptable to engage in phenomenological research of lived experience—somebody else's, of course—it is largely only fem-inist scholars who have stressed the importance of fully integrating the knower in all her vulnerabilities. Morin insists on reminding us that life is not confined to one or two disciplines, and his life involves, among other pursuits, movies, house-hunting, his wife's asthma attacks, pets, conferences, friendships, pub-lishers, and the occasional overindulgence at dinner. A philosophy of life can-not exclude these moments from its purview.

The pretense of objectivity unsullied by the contingency of life has never been something Morin aspired to. In fact, he has been actively working on dis-mantling it. He has also been aware that this academic front has all too often acted a cover for immature emotionality and self-deception. Morin breaks away forcefully from the reductive image of the intellectual as a disembodied brain with a huge ego (which goes unacknowledged, of course, given the stress on objectivity), and opens himself up to us in his work and his actions, for scrutiny, exploration, and appreciation, showing himself to us in the full range of his life experiences. As Maturana and Varela remind us, everything that is said is said by *somebody* (Maturana & Varela, 1987). In traditional academic discourse and inquiry, the focus was on the elimination of that "somebody" in search of the "God's eye view from Nowhere." As we read Morin, he shows us who the "somebody" is and provides us with an example of "embodied" inquiry and personal reflection. With Morin, the "somebody" is not hidden. The inquirer is not artificially excised from the inquiry.

The personal exploration of his journals has, at times, led us deeply into Morin's psyche in ways that would be inconceivable for most traditional social scientists, for whom vulnerability is not generally considered a virtue. Indeed, what is perhaps overlooked is that most social scientists, particularly those who express themselves only in the confines of the professional journal, are simply unable to give voice to the whole of their life and experience. It is generally not part of the education of the social scientist, of the researcher, to understand him or herself, to be able to explore his or her own personal involvement in the research, to document that process and reflect on it, to explore the extent to which the "subjective" and the "objective" co-create each other, let alone deeply question the underlying assumption of his or her work. Autobiography and self-reflection are an awkward endeavor in social science. They are often looked upon with suspicion mixed with grudging admiration. In his journals, Morin is modeling a process of self-inquiry that is also always holographic because it always occurs within a planetary context—and one might paraphrase Morin by saying that he lives in a planetary culture, and the planetary culture lives inside him.

Social science is comfortable with the context of *justification*, not the context of *discovery* (Montuori, 2006). Social scientists present themselves by proposing a position, backed up with empirical data and/or a theoretical framework. We are never privy to the actual process of inquiry itself, to the ups and downs of the research, the blind alleys, the mistakes, the insights, dialogues, and the creative process, unless we read popular (auto-) biographies. In *Journal d'un Livre* (Morin, 1994a), the journal Morin kept while writing *Pour Sortir du XX siecle*, and earlier in *Le Vif du Sujet*, we find remarkable insights into the creative process and the life of a thinker, struggling to fight off the tendency for dispersion, to do, read, experience too much, and lose direction in the process. And yet the very dispersion, although painful for the author, is one of the things that makes Morin such a unique thinker, through his ability to later integrate a broad range of experiences, theoretical perspectives, and insights and the way he shows us how to think about them.

Along with the deeply personal, Morin also dived into the profoundly public, through his closely followed public pronouncements on a variety of issues, whether his impassioned rejection of the Algerian war (Le Sueur, 2003), the events of 1968 in Paris (Morin, Lefort, & Castoriadis, 1968), his advocacy for Turkey's entry into the EU, or, more recently, his writings on the Israel-Palestine question and his role in French environmentalism. A few weeks after the election of Nicolas Sarkozy in 2007, Morin was invited to discuss France's environmental policy with him. Morin is without question part of that dying breed, the public intellectual. His recent critique of Israeli policies toward the Palestinians have led to several court cases triggered by lurid accusations of anti-semitism, and an eventual exoneration. In 2006, this led to the publication of *Le monde moderne et la question juive* [The modern world and the Jewish question], in which, among other things, he stresses the importance of differentiating between anti-semitism and critiques of the Israeli government's policies toward Palestinians (Morin, 2006b). At 86, Morin is still very much a public intellectual, involved in television debates, publishing regular op-ed articles in France's leading newspapers, dialoguing with one of France's leading ecologists (Morin & Hulot, 2007), and also being a member of the French president's prestigious committee on ecology.

Complexity

Morin's vital involvement in intellectual life has also occurred through a series of major conferences and dialogues with scientists, artists, and philosophers. Most notable perhaps is the conference documented in the three volume *L'Unité de l'homme* [Human Unity] (Morin & Piattelli Palmarini, 1978), a multidisciplinary dialogue among primatologists, biologists, neuroscientists, anthropologists, cyberneticists, sociologists, and a variety of other natural and social scientists. This extremely rich series of dialogues, orchestrated by Morin and the Italian cognitive scientist Massimo Piattelli-Palmarini, represents an important step toward Morin's transdisciplinary approach. It goes beyond interdisciplinarity, which involves using the methods of one discipline to inform another, to draw on multiple disciplines while actually challenging the disciplinary organization of knowledge, and the reductive/disjunctive way of thinking that makes up what Morin was to call the "paradigm of simplicity." Transdisciplinarity aims for a different way of thinking, and a different way of organizing knowledge. Several of Morin's books find him in dialogues with social and natural scientists, from astrophysicists to biologists to sociologists and philosophers. To give an idea of the breadth involved, Morin is featured prominently in books on the implications of the work of Ilya Prigogine (Spire, 1999); in a volume on complexity theory with Francisco Varela, Brian Goodwin, Stuart Kauffman and Prigogine, among others (Benkirane, 2006); debates with Réné Thom and Michel Serres (Morin, 1983); in a dialogue on memory and responsibility with

Emmanuel Levinas (de Saint Cheron, 2000); in dialogue with astrophysicists Michel Cassé (Cassé & Morin, 2003) and Hubert Reeves (Morin & Le Moigne, 1999); and most recently ecologist Michel Hulot (Morin & Hulot, 2007). I mention this in particular because of the recent perception in the United States that French intellectual "impostors" have misappropriated and misrepresented science. In Morin's case, this is certainly not true. In fact, we find that he actually contributes to the articulation of the implications of the new sciences for scientists themselves (Roux-Rouquié, 2002; Westbroek, 2004). The proceedings of the prestigious Colloque de Cerisy, which includes Henri Atlan, Cornelius Castoriadis, Gianluca Bocchi, Sergio Manghi, Mauro Ceruti, and Isabelle Stengers, among others, give further indication of Morin's breadth and influence (Bougnoux, Le Moigne, & Proulx, 1990). His edited book on education, *Relier les connaissances* [Reconnecting Knowledges] (Morin, 1999b), includes an essay by Paul Ricoeur among others.

Le Paradigme Perdu [Paradigm Lost], published in 1973, represents the first step toward the integration that was later to culminate in the multivolume *Method*. For Morin, healing the split between the natural and social sciences was essential. His multidimensional approach to human nature—and to inquiry in general—could not abide with the human/nature split. In the social sciences there was either the quantitative approach found in sociology (what Sorokin called "quantophrenia"), generally anemic attempts to copy the method of physics, or the more philosophically inclined tendency to reject anything remotely associated with the natural sciences as reductive, as "scientism" or "biologism." In natural science the almost complete absence of reflection on the role of the inquirer created massive blind spots science itself was unable to address in its most rigid configuration. As Dortier points out, *Le Paradigme Perdu* was written before sociobiology and evolutionary psychology became trendy, but it deserves to be read not just out of respect and historical interest for a book that was ahead of its time, but because Morin outlined an important agenda and way of thinking about the issues that is still extremely fruitful (Dortier, 2006). And this is in many ways Morin's central contribution—to point out that there are human problems, such as the human/nature or two-culture split, that must be approached with a radically different way of thinking, a way of thinking that, as Morin states, is not disjunctive (either/or), but connects, without the Hegelian assumption that the dialectic will always lead to a new synthesis.

First in *Le Paradigme Perdu*, then in the massive *Method* (Morin, 1985, 1986, 1991, 1992a, 2003, 2006a), Morin tackles this "en-cyclo-pedic" task by literally circulating knowledge between the disciplines and opening up a new way of approaching inquiry and knowledge. Around the time *Le Paradigme Perdu* was being written, and until quite recently, postmodern thinkers like Lyotard, Habermas, and others were highly critical of the integration of natural and social sciences and against systems theoretical approaches in particular

(Lyotard, 1984). Lechte's (1994): summary of Lyotard's position is typical of the way systems theoretical approaches are summarily dealt with in much post-modern discourse:

> For the systems theorist, human beings are part of a homogeneous, stable, theoretically knowable, and therefore, predictable system. Knowledge is the means of controlling the system. Even if perfect knowledge does not yet exist, the equation: the greater the knowledge the greater the power over the system is, for the systems theorist, irrefutable. (p. 248)

Morin saw the enormous potential of these new approaches while recognizing their limitations, and he refused to be limited by ideological boundaries. In the process he developed his own complex interpretation of systems theory, information theory, and cybernetics, designed to connect the various dimensions of human inquiry, separated as they were in their own worlds and disciplines, refusing to communicate with each other. Ironically, *Method* begins with an extensive discussion of the relationship between order and disorder, the key role of emergence, unpredictability, and uncertainty in his approach to complexity, and the importance of the prefix "re-" as in re-organization, re-thinking, and so on, suggesting ongoing process and change (Morin, 2005c). Morin could not be as easily dismissed as traditional sociological systems thinkers such as Talcott Parsons. In the United States, the very fact that he did not fit neatly into one camp and could not be reduced to some simple category (systems theorist, structuralist, post-modernist, post-structuralist) has led to any number of misinformed assessments of his work, particularly because until recently only a very small number of his books have been translated into English, giving a very partial view of a multidimensional body of work.

The 6-volume *Method* is Morin's magnum opus, a remarkable and seemingly inexhaustible treasure trove of insights, reflection, and a real manual for those who are interested in broadening the nature of human inquiry. *Method* integrates the rich and diverse elements of Morin's journey and provides the reader with an alternative to the traditional assumptions and methods of inquiry of our time. Morin's method outlines a way of approaching inquiry that does not reduce or separate, and does justice to the complexity of life and experience. In his sociopolitical works, such as his prescient studies on the USSR and totalitarianism, on the nature and concept of Europe, and his "manifesto for the 21st century," *Homeland Earth* (Morin & Kern, 1999), Morin applied this method to the planetary crisis in what he calls this "planetary iron age."

Most recently, Morin has produced, in some cases at the request of UNESCO and the French government, a series of books and conferences addressing the application of complex thought in educational contexts (Morin, 2001b). This is part of his ongoing quest to address the crucial issue of preparing human beings to tackle the challenge of complexity. It is a particularly tough challenge because the level Morin is addressing is largely invisible precisely because it does address only the *content* of our thoughts as much as the *organization* of our thinking through, for instance, a disjunctive logic that creates binary oppositions, and therefore organizes our thinking in such a way that we approach the world with an organizing framework of either/or. Rather than focus exclusively on challenging binary oppositions, Morin digs deep to excavate the underlying paradigm that generates those oppositions, and articulates a generative paradigm of complexity that offers a different point of departure. Interestingly, Morin's work on education has found particular resonance in Latin America (particularly Brazil and Colombia), Italy, and Spain.

In over 50 years of writing and passionate participation in French, European, and planetary culture, Morin has shown us the way toward a richer, deeper appreciation of and participation in life. Our present way of thinking, feeling, and being, Morin proposes, is deeply problematic: It reduces, separates, and opposes. Morin points us beyond this way of thinking and toward a paradigm of complexity: toward a way of thinking and being that does not mutilate life, but allows us to live it more fully by being more present to the complexities, paradoxes, tragedies, joys, failures, and successes. He points us toward a way of thinking that is not disembodied and abstract, but rich in feeling, intuition, and connection to the larger social and historical context. A thought that is holographic and contextual, showing us how we are embedded in time and space. But a thought that is also transformative, self-eco-re-organizing, by including all of who we are and indeed stretching our understanding of who we are and pointing us toward new possibilities.

Morin's work has gradually led to the development of a transdisciplinary approach to inquiry. Going beyond the fragmentation and hyper-specialization too often promoted in academia, Morin has approached a variety of subjects normally confined in isolated disciplines and brought to them his own complex sensibility, while at the same time, in the process of immersing himself in his inquiry, he has been able to draw from the subjects a further stimulus and impetus for his own conception of transdisciplinary inquiry. It is this kind of generative loop that is one of the trademarks of Morin's complex thought and his complex practice of inquiry. It is to be hoped that in the coming years, Morin's work will receive the long overdue attention it deserves in the English-speaking world, and assist us in the challenge of living in an ever-increasingly complex, uncertain, and ambiguous world.

INTRODUCTION: ON COMPLEXITY

This short volume contains some key essays by French thinker Edgar Morin on the subject of complexity, and specifically on what Morin calls *complex thought*. The earliest essay, "Complex Pattern and Design," was written in 1976, and the other essays date back to the 1980s and 1990s. One might seriously wonder what such a collection of essays has to offer beyond an interesting historical document of a thinker who was considerably ahead of his time. The last 15 years or so have seen a tremendous outpouring of books and articles on complexity. When Morin wrote these pages, the term *complexity* was not popular. It wasn't an intellectual trend, there was no Santa Fe Institute, there were no popularizing works explaining the relevance of complexity theory to business, health care, or group process. So why, when complexity is all the rage and we are overwhelmed with information, new books, new perspectives, new ideas on complexity, go back to these essays, some of which were written more than 20 years ago?

One of the patterns that connects Morin's considerable contributions in such varied fields as biology and cinema, sociology and ecology, is *a particularly generative way of approaching the subject matter*. It's not a methodology, in the sense of a new research methodology like action research. The issue is premethodological. It is an issue of what Morin calls *method*, understood in the broadest sense of the word, as a "way" or "path laid down in walking." As the noted Italian family systems therapist Mara Selvini Palazzoli wrote (Selvini Palazzoli, 1990),

> As Edgar Morin has put it so shrewdly, "the method emerges from the research." Originally, he points out, the word method meant path; it is only in traveling that the right method appears. (p. xiv)

How do we engage in inquiry? How do we think about the world, and more specifically, how do we approach research? Above all, how do we organize knowledge? How can we live and think in a pluralistic universe, with complexity, uncertainty, and ambiguity? Iain Chambers, who has written extensively on the subject of cultural complexity, writes:

> The idea of both lived and intellectual complexity, of Edgar Morin's *"la pensée complexe,"* introduces us to a social ecology of being and knowledge. Here both thought and everyday activities move in the realm of uncertainty. Linear argument and certainty break down as we find ourselves orbiting in a perpetual paradox around the wheel of being: we bestow sense, yet we can never be certain in our proclamations. The idea of cultural complexity, most

sharply on display in the arabesque patterns of the modern metropolis—and that includes Lagos as well as London, Beijing, and Buenos Aires—weakens earlier schemata and paradigms; it destabilizes and decenters previous theories and sociologies. Here the narrow arrow of linear progress is replaced by the open spiral of hybrid cultures, contaminations, and what Edward Said recently referred to as "atonal ensembles." The city suggests creative disorder, an instructive confusion, an interpolating space in which the imagination carries you in every direction, even toward the previously unthought. (1993, p. 189)

In the tradition of such writers as Bachelard, Bateson, and others, Morin's work is a sustained epistemological reflection on the implications of the scientific and cultural revolution of the 20th century for our organization of, and relationship with, knowledge (Bachelard, 2002; Bateson, 2002; Capra, 1996; Taylor, 2003).

The term *organization of knowledge* may suggest a particularly abstruse and arcane endeavor of relevance only to specialists, and of absolutely no relevance for the way human beings lead their lives. But the organization of knowledge has enormously far-reaching consequences. The implications are obvious in the way we lead our daily lives (Kegan, 1998), the history and development of social science (Fay, 1996) and in the most pressing political and religious issues we face today (Bernstein, 2005). Despite the apparent resistance to this process of "thinking about thinking," and the contribution of the above-mentioned authors, Morin's contribution in this area is of great importance. The question is not just *what* we know, but *how* we know, and *how* we organize our knowledge.

The key elements of the organization of knowledge in the West go far back in history. The work of Aristotle and Descartes is central. Aristotle developed a "logic," providing us with concepts such as the law of identity and the excluded middle. In his *Discourse on Method*, Descartes (Descartes, 1954) explored the basic *laws of thinking* and fashioned them into the foundations for inquiry. Descartes spoke of a *method* and of *Rules for the direction of the mind*. In other words, Descartes was providing us with an orientation for the way we think, a focus on reduction, simplification, and clarity. What Descartes proposed as rules for the direction of mind has, coupled with Aristotle's logic, become the foundation for "good thinking," and institutionalized in the organization of universities. There we find the same increasing specialization in departments, literally the splitting up into smallest possible parts, and the creation of strong boundaries based on three axioms of classical logic (Nicolescu, 2002).

The limitations of this kind of thinking are becoming increasingly apparent. None of the sciences offer us a way to integrate all the tremendous quantities of information and knowledge generated in the various disciplines and subdisciplines. This is extremely problematic for at least two reasons. First, with increasing specialization, the "big questions" are simply not asked and addressed anymore. Second, action in the world cannot be confined to knowledge drawn from one discipline. For example, the future of "developing countries" cannot be viewed exclusively from the neatly quantifiable perspective of economics. As Morin states, such a concept of development is underdeveloped. Another example is that innovation in industry cannot be reduced to one individual having a bright idea. There are any number of extremely bright and creative individuals in organizations with good ideas—and organizational bureaucracies are notorious for squashing new ideas. So the process of organizational innovation is multidimensional—it has individual psychological (personality, cognitive) dimensions, but also group and organizational dimensions, not to mention an economic dimension. The implication is that fostering creativity and innovation in organizations cannot simply be confined to giving individuals "creativity tools." The process needs to be systemic, and more than cross-disciplinary, it should be transdisciplinary, in order to, among other things, include the inquirer in the inquiry, the innovator in the innovation (Purser & Montuori, 1999). Real understanding and effective action therefore require an approach that is not dictated by disciplinary boundaries but emerges from the needs of the inquiry.

As I have argued elsewhere (Montuori, 2005a), drawing on Morin's work, transdisciplinarity can be summarized as requiring:

1. A focus that is *inquiry-driven* rather than discipline driven. This in no way involves a rejection of disciplinary knowledge, but the development of knowledge that is pertinent to the inquiry for the purposes of action in the world.

2. A stress on *the construction of knowledge* through an appreciation of *the meta-paradigmatic dimension*—in other words, the underlying assumptions that form the paradigm through which disciplines and perspectives construct knowledge, Disciplinary knowledge generally does not question its paradigmatic assumptions.

3. An understanding of *the organization of knowledge*, isomorphic at the cognitive and the institutional level, the history of reduction and disjunction (what Morin calls "simple thought"), and the importance of contextualization and connection (or "complex thought").

4. *The integration of the knower in the process of inquiry*, which means that rather than attempting to eliminate the knower, the effort becomes one of acknowledging and making transparent the knower's assumptions and the process through which s/he constructs knowledge.

As Morin wrote:

> The observer should not just practice a method that permits her to shift from
> one perspective to another. . . . She also needs a method to access a meta-
> point of view on the diverse points of view, including her own point of view.
> (p. 179)

Morin, and many other thinkers including Fay, Code, and Collins, have shown
how at the sociological level, dichotomies have marked the history of Western
thought in the form of opposing movements such as atomism and holism
(Code, 1991; Collins, 1998; Fay, 1996). The history of ideas reflects ways of
thinking that are in turn also reflected in the disciplinary nature of academia
and research. *The organization of knowledge is isomorphic at the level of thought, the
history of ideas, and disciplines.* There is an isomorphism between what Morin
calls the reductive/disjunctive "simple thought" that has characterized much of
Western history, and the organization of knowledge in universities, where
knowledge is broken down in ever smaller disciplines and subdisciplines and
specializations, with increasingly impermeable borders. One finds a disjunctive
logic that places a scholar either in one discipline or another—but never in
both. With some exceptions, one can usually not be both A *and* B, both a psy-
chologist *and* a sociologist, for instance. Wilshire's disturbing research has illus-
trated the dynamics of "purity" and "pollution" associated with university disciplines (Montuori & Purser, 1999; Wilshire, 1990). Morin is pointing in a new
direction, proposing his en-cyclo-pedic method that circulates knowledge
between disciplines, and proposes the paradigm of complexity not as a
panacea, not as a solution to the problem, but as a way of approaching the
organization of our thinking and thinking about organization.

One recurring theme in the more sophisticated recent discussions of complexity, whether in the sciences, management and organizational theory, or the
social sciences in general, is that reductive/analytic approaches to issues are
unable to account for, and give an adequate understanding of, complex, interconnected phenomena. Reductive approaches isolate phenomena from their
environment and operate with a disjunctive logic of either/or. I have suggested
this kind of thinking can be found writ large in the organization of knowledge
in universities, with departments focusing studies in ever greater hyper-specialization. Sadly there is little or no effort to *connect* the knowledge gathered in the
different departments, or to elaborate how the knowledge gained in different
disciplines might be integrated in practical applications in the world. Many
popular (pseudo-)holistic approaches that define themselves in opposition to
reductionism and reject "parts" in favor of "wholes," "analysis" in favor of "synthesis," and "control" in favor of "emergence," almost inevitably end up being
vague and ineffectual feel-good New Age nostrums rather than serious efforts

to address complexity, wholeness, and interconnectedness (Montuori, 2006). Morin's trenchant critique of this form of holism—which is the direct opposite of reductionism and itself a product of disjunctive thinking—is one of the ways his work makes such an important contribution to the development of a new way of thinking and a new approach to inquiry (Morin, 2008).

Another key dimensions of Morin's work is that it recognizes the ambiguity and uncertainty that is the hallmark of 20th century science and human experience. Complex thought leads us to a way of thinking—and being in the world—that recognizes the inescapable dimension of uncertainty, and views it as an opportunity for creativity and the development of new perspectives, rather than primarily a source of anxiety.

Order and Disorder: Chaosmos

In his masterpiece *Method*, Morin introduces a key element to his thinking: the dethroning of King Order. In the first volume (Morin, 1992a), he addresses this through an extensive discussion of scientific developments in the last centuries. Scientists today are in agreement that we are in the middle of a scientific revolution. In the words of theoretical physicist Paul Davies (1989):

> For three centuries, science has been dominated by the Newtonian and thermodynamic paradigms, which present the universe as either a sterile machine, or in a state of degeneration and decay. Now there is the paradigm of the creative universe, which recognizes the progressive, innovative character of physical processes. The new paradigm emphasizes the collective, cooperative, and organizational aspects of nature; its perspective is synthetic and holistic rather than analytic and reductionistic. (p. 2)

The paradigm of the creative universe. It is not just a different understanding of the universe, but the need for a different way of thinking about, and inquiring into, the universe that emerges. As Davies makes very clear, we are looking at a new perspective on the world, one that is "is synthetic and holistic rather than analytic and reductionist," and recognizes "the collective, cooperative, and organizational aspects of nature." Davies is describing a move away from the classical scientific worldview toward a view that points to Morin's articulation of complexity. The phenomena science is exploring require a different way of thinking. Indeed, in his works spanning such traditional disciplines as sociology, biology, political science, ecology, and psychology, Morin has shown how we can fruitfully apply a new way of thinking to human life as a whole.

True scientific revolutions amount to more than new discoveries: They alter the concepts on which science and our whole view of the world is based. Historians will distinguish three levels of enquiry in the study of matter. The first is Newtonian mechanics—the triumph of necessity. The second is equilibrium thermodynamics—the triumph of chance. Now there is a third level, emerging from the study of far-from-equilibrium systems (Davies, 1989, p. 83).

The Newtonian revolution represented the first real coherent triumph of what we now call science. With his *Principia*, published in 1687, Newton presented in the form of mathematical equations the three laws that govern the motion of material bodies. Newton's work was particularly important because it presented Universal Laws of Nature. These laws seemed to give a window into the functioning and nature of Nature itself. Particularly powerful in Newton's work was its focus on prediction, order, and determinism. In the words of Davies (1989, p. 11), with Newton "the entire cosmos is reduced to a gigantic clockwork mechanism, with each component slavishly and unfailingly executing its preprogrammed instructions to mathematical precision."

The laws and principles created the foundation for general theories and predictions that could be tested through experiments. These experiments, conducted following the scientific method, consisted of breaking systems down to their simplest components, a method now referred to as *reductionism*. This reflected an assumption that the world was made of basic building blocks called atoms. The underlying assumption was that these atoms exist in isolation from their environment, and that knowledge of the behavior of the atoms could be used to predict the future of the system as a whole.

Two fundamental things make up the Newtonian world: matter and energy. Matter and energy exist in the emptiness of absolute space and time—the "sterile machine" Davies mentions. Matter is composed of atoms and even subatomic particles such as electrons and protons. Knowing the location, mass, and velocity of all the particles in the universe, it would be possible to predict the future. With progressive improvement in scientific knowledge, in other words, it was believed that eventually it would be possible to predict every event. The Newtonian world was therefore deterministic. Every event *had* to happen *by necessity*. Once set in motion, the universe unfolds following precise laws. The assumption was that fundamentally, the universe is governed by simplicity and simple rules. There is an unquestionable order to the universe, and anything we consider disorder or complexity was simply a function of our limited knowledge. Simplicity, predictability, and determinism were central to the Newtonian worldview.

The Newtonian world was also "reversible." This means that "time exists merely as a parameter for gauging the interval between events. Past and future have no real significance. Nothing actually *happens*" (Davies, 1989, p. 14). This is a particularly interesting feature that defies common sense, but made perfect sense in the Newtonian world. The Newtonian world is therefore a "clean machine," like a clockwork. Interestingly, it reflects the same static view of the world before Newton, which was considered a perfect, pre-ordained, God-given hierarchical order: Nothing actually happens, because the Laws of Nature are the Laws of God, and these Laws are perfect, therefore no change occurs, is necessary, or even possible.

The Newtonian worldview had very clear implications for our thinking. The power of prediction and control that the scientific method provided was staggering. The technology driving the Industrial Revolution was the result of the application of the new scientific method. Who, in the middle of this explosion of human power, could argue with it? The social sciences and the management sciences wanted to import the scientific method, in order to enjoy the same legitimacy as real sciences. Being a real science was defined largely by the capacity for prediction and control. The scientific method led to technology and industry, which in turn led to progress.

The notion of progress became central to modernity. The belief was that the scientific method offered a way to get at truth in a manner that was empirical, testable, and gave the user power. It's important to understand that before the scientific method was applied, people simply did not think this way. Before the scientific method, what was considered the "highest" or most evolved form of thinking on a social level was a mixture of Aristotle, the encyclopedic Greek philosopher who had written about everything from logic to biology, and the writings of St. Thomas which informed theology, drawn from the Bible. In this pre-modern view, Aristotle and the Bible were seen as unquestionable sources of wisdom. The concept of experiment that would give empirical proof as to whether a particular hypothesis was, or was not the case, was unheard of.

The scientific method led to a shift from a more passive reception of already given knowledge to the active acquisition of new knowledge. This led to a focus on several key areas, which can be represented in the following oppositions, the latter term indicating what the new method rejected:

- Objective knowledge of objects in the exterior world, rather than subjective knowledge of interior moods, opinions, experiences, and so on;
- Quantification, and therefore "objective" data that could be measured as opposed to qualitative data that is "subjective" and cannot be measured;
- Reductionism, or a focus on parts rather than wholes (holism);
- Determinism—or finding laws of cause and effect that determine events as opposed to chance events that cannot be predicted by laws (contingency);
- Certainty, rather than uncertainty;
- Universal knowledge (applicable anywhere and everywhere) rather than particular, local knowledge (applicable only to certain specific settings);

- One right way of looking at a situation, rather than a multiplicity of perspectives, and the search for that one right way;
- Either/or thinking, borrowed from Aristotle, which rejects any form of ambiguity or paradox.

The Decaying Machine

The second revolution in science was ushered in by the second law of thermodynamics. It addressed the issue of irreversibility. Irreversibility is a very basic feature of the world from our everyday point of view. You can't become young again, unbreak an egg, "take back" an unkind comment, or "unlose" your lost keys (you can find them in the *future*, of course). Literally we can't go back in time to undo or reverse an action. And yet the Newtonian world was "reversible." Time as such played no role in it. Everything essentially stayed the same, and the movie could be played forward or backward with no visible difference.

With the second law, Rudolf Clausius in the middle of the 19th century developed the familiar concept of *entropy*. In a nutshell, the second law of thermodynamics states that "in a closed system, entropy never decreases," where entropy is defined as energy that is unavailable for work. Entropy is the disorder or randomness in a system. So as a machine worked, some energy became unavailable for work. What this brought us is a view of the universe as a decaying machine, a closed, mechanical system struggling against the forces of corrosion and decay. A machine, yes, but a machine that is running down and inexorably moving toward the end. Time was introduced into the picture, and its role was essentially to tear away at the primal perfection.

As a machine worked over time, it would gradually lose energy. But along with this loss of energy, there also seemed to be another process. Decay was not the only direction time seemed to lead to. There was a parallel time that seemed to defy the universe's winding down. It was a time not of machines, but of life.

DARWIN'S REVOLUTION

It was Charles Darwin who added a completely new wrinkle to our understanding of the world (Ceruti, 2008). Before the emergence of science, it was generally thought that the world had been created in 4004 B.C.E., and everything on the planet was the result of God's plan. This meant that every creature on the planet had been placed there by God, in the "Great Chain of Being," and nothing had really "changed," because that would mean a deviation from God's plan.

Darwin, on the other hand, suggested that life on the Earth had started quite simply and evolved into more complex forms.

Darwin's world was not Newton's world, or Clausius's world (Bocchi & Ceruti, 2002). Newton's world was static. Clausius's was running down. Darwin's seemed to be getting more and more complex, indeed, "evolving." Darwin's original image of the evolutionary process was very much a product of his times. The concept of *progress*, which was very much in the air as Darwin was doing his research, suggested that science, technology, and human reason would lead us to a better world, free of disease, poverty, and so on. Darwin's concept of evolution was immediately translated by many as being synonymous with progress. If life is an evolutionary process, meaning that life on this planet evolved from simple micro-organisms to complex creatures like human beings, then evolution signified a progression from simple to complex, from primitive to superior, and consequently, there is a form of progress built into the natural world.

This view of evolution as linear progress, with all its tantalizing implications for social systems, has been challenged as simplistic by some and fundamentally misguided by others. It has been argued that just because life on this planet has evolved, reproduced, and changed, this is not a clear indication at all that it's getting somehow "better." But regardless of these arguments, Darwin presented a third scientific perspective—neither perfect machine, nor decaying machine, but rather an explosion of life, reproducing itself and changing as it does so. And in this process, time played an active, creative role, because things changed as they reproduced, and as they came into contact with each other. The principle of natural selection suggested that interaction played a central role in evolution.

From the Clockwork World, where Order was King, to a Decaying World, to a Creative World. The crucial difference in the development of these different understandings of the world lies in the relationship between Order and Disorder. And the new articulation of this relationship between Order and Disorder, traditionally framed in terms either/or, is central to Morin's work and takes up a good part of the first volume of *Method*.

In Newton's world, Order reigned, and what we perceived as Disorder was simply the result of our human ignorance. We simply were not yet aware of the Laws governing the phenomena we called disordered, confused, ambiguous. This is also the Laplacean universe, where virtual omniscience is the ideal.

With Clausius and the second law of thermodynamics, we find that Order and Organization move toward Disorder.

With Darwin, and the new developments in physics, Morin proposes a key tetragram that shows how the interactions of order and disorder lie at the heart of organization. Order, disorder, and organization have a complex relationship through interaction (Morin, 1981).

Organization without disorder leads to a sterile, homogenous system where no change and innovation is possible. Complete disorder without order precludes organization. Only with the interaction of order and disorder, is an organization possible that remains open to change, growth, and possibilities (Morin, 2007).

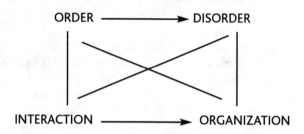

One of the key differences is that entropy applies to closed systems, but life on earth is not a closed system. In an open system, there are processes that actually create order. The concept of "open system" is vital to understanding the shift to the creative universe. The first volume of Morin's *Method* introduces in some considerable depth the implications of this shift. Rather than assuming that there is a pre-established order—whether God-given or somehow intrinsic to nature, Morin explores in great depth the importance of the generative, emergent relationship between order and disorder.

Order, Disorder, and Self-Organization

In the traditional Newtonian scientific paradigm, order was King, privileged above disorder, chaos, and "noise" (Morin, 1992a). Our understanding of the relationship between order and disorder was in terms of a binary opposition, and indeed a hierarchical binary opposition. Disorder was viewed as a function of human ignorance, something that would, eventually, with better knowledge, be integrated in the larger master-plan.

One of the most interesting shifts in recent scientific thinking, in particular because of the sciences of chaos and complexity, has been a deeper understanding of the mutually constitutive relationship between order and disorder, information and noise. This shift also reflects a transition from a fundamentally static view of the world to one that is process oriented. Rather than seeing order as fundamental and unchanging, we are now seeing an ongoing process of order-disorder-interaction-organization that is the hallmark of self-organization (Morin, 2007). As Taylor (2003, p. 121) writes, "disorder does not simply destroy order, structure, and organization, but is also a condition of their formation and reformation." The interaction of order and disorder can be generative of new forms of organization, and any order is the result of an ongoing process, not of pre-established forms.

Self-organization has been defined variously as making meaning out of randomness (Atlan, 1986), or the spontaneous emergence of a coordinated and collective behavior in a population of elements. One of the key aspects of self-organization is the creation of order out of chaos, the integration of elements perceived as disorder into a larger, more encompassing organization. We might think of paradigms in science as an analogy. What is inside the paradigm is considered order, what is outside is disorder. Anomalies on the edge of the paradigm, what the paradigm cannot account for, may initially seem like noise, disorderly phenomena that cannot be accounted for. Indeed, the history of chaos theory itself shows how turbulent phenomena such as water flowing from a faucet were rejected out of hand as subjects of study for the longest time because they seemed simply inexplicable. Yet it is the study of these anomalies that led to the development of the new science of dynamical systems, also known as *chaos theory*. In this sense, chaos theory as a field of study was itself a self-organizing process, the spontaneous emergence of a coordinated and collective behavior in a population of elements (researchers), making meaning out of (apparent) randomness.

The term *self-organization* refers to a spontaneous emergence of collaborative behavior among elements in a system. The whole idea of what we might call Newtonian organization, or the Machine Metaphor of organization was that the existing order that had been created was perfect, and workers were there to implement it. In Tayloristic (Newtonian) organizations, it was spontaneity at all costs, as it involved a breakdown in the established order. Self-organization, on the other hand, involves the emergence of order out of spontaneous interactions in response to disorder. It is interesting to note that Taylor insisted on making sure individual workers did not communicate, or form into groups. Their whole purpose was to perform their pre-established isolated assembly-line function. Spontaneous interactions were precisely what Taylor wanted to avoid, and the workers were organized from the outside, never self-organized.

Morin has argued that a more accurate and inclusive way to describe the process of self-organization in open, dynamical systems is as "self-eco-re-organizing systems" (Morin, 1990, 2005c, 2008) A system does not merely organize itself, independently of its environment. The environment is in the system, which is in the environment. A family is in society, and society is in the family (culturally, economically, through the media, and so on). But a system does not merely self-eco-organize. It self-eco-*re*-organizes, as we shall see below (Morin, 2005c).

The order out of disorder that emerges in an open system's interaction with its environment is subject to fluctuation. When certain levels of fluctuation are created by increasing complexity, a critical or bifurcation point is reached. At that point the system can move in any one of several directions until a new and more complex order may be established after a period of turbulence. If a higher order of organization does not emerge, the system returns to a previous, lower level of organization. Many developmental psychologists report a similar pattern for evolutionary transformation (Guidano, 1987; Kegan, 1982). We might therefore think of evolutionary transformation as an ongoing process of self-eco-re-organization.

Re-: The Importance of Time, History, and Process

Although the Newtonian view was "reversible," where time did not play a role, in the new scientific view, time, history, and process play a key role. As the Italian philosophers of science Bocchi and Ceruti write, during this century science has come to recognize that organisms are, to a large extent, their history (Bocchi & Ceruti, 2002). An organization today is the result of its history—of the choices, decisions, and events that have occurred in its lifespan. To say that one is one's history does not mean, on the other hand, that one is *determined* by that history on some inexorable future. On the contrary. Whereas the traditional scientific view was deterministic, the new one is much more focused on creativity, as Morin's Re- suggests. And history is where creativity happened, in the form of contingencies, of surprises, of the unforeseen. Unforeseen events can shape our lives in ways we never expected. This was Morin's focus in his early sociological work, of course: not the universal laws, but the inclusion of contingency, chance, of *events*. Inquiry therefore has to be able to address uncertainty and ambiguity, but not simply as demonstrations of our lack of knowledge. In this view, contingency, the out of the ordinary, and ambiguity are sources of change, of *a creative process*.

Every system, whether individual or a corporation, is also an organization. But an organization is not static. And organization is always re-organization. Organization therefore is always a process, not something that is fixed and once and for all. In fact, Morin has even coined the neologism "organiz-action" to stress this (Morin, 1992a). Any organization that is completely unchangeable is unable to adapt to changes in the environment, and unable to create anything new. The prefix "re-" is therefore a key indicator that organization is not static, but a process of constant, ongoing, self-eco-re-organization.

At the same time, just as the world is increasingly confronting us with the unexpected, we can also generate the unexpected ourselves. Creativity involves those acts that are unexpected and therefore produce something defined as new, original, and unusual that is also considered valuable and, to a greater or lesser extent, of lasting value. For Morin the unexpected is indeed a source of hope. History is replete with the unexpected. Who could have predicted the fall of the Soviet Union, for instance? Morin is urging us to befriend the unexpected and inviting us to learn how to live in a world that is not ruled by one overarching order, but where freedom, spontaneity, surprise, and the unexpected are the order of the day. Classical science assumed all systems were fundamentally stable and in equilibrium, and chaotic systems, far from equilibrium were the exception. The new sciences of chaos and complexity theories show us that equilibrium systems are in fact the exception. The world is full of ambiguity and uncertainty, and Morin is pointing us to ways of thinking through and living with that ambiguity.

The Need for a New Way of Thinking

How can we best approach a world that is full of uncertainty, complexity, and ambiguity? Are we prepared for this tremendous challenge? How can we address the uncertainty, complexity, and ambiguity of the "planetary era," in which our remarkable interconnectedness has led us to face a world we can barely recognize? Alvin Toffler spoke of *Future Shock* 30 years ago, and it seems we are now in the middle of it (Toffler, 1984). My colleague Dan Crowe recently told me that the students in his graduate course on leadership at a university in Georgia balked at the suggestion that they should read *The Economist* and familiarize themselves with global economics. Noticing their reluctance to take on this assignment, my colleague pointed out to them that global events, no matter how remote they may seem, do have profound repercussions in the daily lives of his students. In fact, the closure of a factory in the Atlanta area had recently cost thousands of jobs that all went to Mexico. We are now, as Morin would say, *planetary citizens*. But it's clear that our educational systems have not prepared us for this condition. And what's more, it's far from clear that there is a sense of urgency about understanding our planetary context. We are simply not prepared for the full implications of a global, interconnected, uncertain world. In fact, it's increasingly obvious that it's painfully difficult to even figure out how to begin to *think* about this world we're living in.

Unraveling the complexities of global economics and its social impact is an enormous challenge. The world is full of uncertainty. We don't know what will happen to our job, our neighborhood and our city, our country. Change is so rapid, and technology in particular is playing such a dramatic role in this acceleration, that we can't in good faith expect things to stay the same for very long. Whereas in previous ages life was arguably relatively simple, predictable, and unambiguous, we are now faced with a different world. But are we equipped to deal with it? Increasingly, the answer is no.

Disturbingly, in times of transition, complexity, uncertainty, or faced with potential or even actual chaos, there is a tendency to seek out absolute foundations, certainty, simplicity, and a framework that will make sense of the world and reduce our anxiety. These frameworks are informed by reductionistic and dualistic thinking that drastically reduce the complexity of the world.

What this means in practice is that in times of great anxiety, human beings often need to reduce the complexity by finding one source to blame for their anxiety and attribute to it all that is wrong (scapegoating). This is accompanied by thinking in dualistic terms: *They* are bad, *we* are good. If you're not for us, you're against us. "They" are the capitalist running dogs, the evil empire, the witches, the Jews, the polluting industries, and so on (Bernstein, 2005; Montuori, 2005b).

Gerald Holton spoke of the "themata," the major recurring themes in the work of creative scientists (Holton, 1988). One of the central themata running through Morin's work is a critique of this kind of simplistic thinking, or "simple thought," in the direct translation from the French. The problems with simple thought are legion. Dualistic thinking creates a classic problem. If I assume that you are evil and I am good, then in the heat of the mission to "defeat evil," anything I do is by definition legitimate and good, and anything you do is bad. But if I am so unwaveringly convinced that I am good—in an "essentialist" way, in the same way that I see you as "essentially" evil—then all my actions become, to some extent, beyond reproach in my battle against the forces of evil. This leads to the phenomenon that Jung called *enantiodromia* whereby we literally become what we hate (Jung, 1976). Examples abound. In order for my democratic country to fight my totalitarian enemy, I must take all precautions, including surveillance of citizens, and the gradual erosion of civil rights, including the right to protest or even disagree with my policies. Anybody who disagrees with me is viewed as aiding and abetting the enemy. In the process of fighting my enemy, I have taken such a drastic stance that the very democracy I am trying to defend is lost in the process, through my own policies, not the actions of the enemy.

Particularly in his more autobiographical accounts, Morin expresses his personal dismay at the way that a certain way of thinking can lead us to demonize "the other," whether communist, capitalist, German, and so on. The other is *reduced* to the crimes committed, and a clean, dualistic separation is made between "us and them." Here we are already in the thick of complexity. It is tempting to say that not reducing Germans after World War II to the Nazi horror is fundamentally excusing them, letting them off the hook. The complex perspective recognizes both the horror and the grandeur and humanity of a people who have, after all, made enormous contributions to Western civilization. It's much easier to say they are somehow evil and leave it at that. It's much harder to see that during a specific period of time, preceded by desperate economic hardship and national humiliation, under the influence of masters of propaganda, and much, much more, Germany fell into an abyss of horror. And that the punitive measures of Versailles themselves contributed to the chaos that led to WW II, a lesson that was learned and led to the Marshall Plan, the remarkable recovery of Germany, Italy, and Japan after the war, and the close bonds with those countries that have lasted to this day.

The example of Germany after WW II is interesting because now very few people if any would take this demonizing, dualistic view of Germany. But at the same time, we see that discussions of Islam in the West often take on a very similar character. The image of the West and particularly the United States and Israel proposed in some Islamic fundamentalist circles is even more appallingly demonizing.

Reductionism is, in such situations, coupled with disjunction, the "us and them" approach. This adds to the simplicity. We do not have to deal with the complexity of the German people, of Islam, of the West. We can simply say they are fundamentally evil and forget about their humanity and their contributions to humanity. And we can also avoid looking into the complexity of our own humanness. We can then avoid addressing our shared humanity, and the very real possibility that we ourselves may be capable of equally horrific behaviors. Indeed, Morin's work on simple thought has clear connections to the classic research on the authoritarian personality (Adorno, Frenkel-Brunswik, Levinson, & Sanford, 1982; Montuori, 2005b). Characteristics such as black and white, dualistic thinking, anti-introspection (unwillingness to look within and explore the full extent of one's humanness, particularly one's weaknesses), and pseudo-conservatism, which involves the tendency to be so extreme and unreflective about preserving what one has that one is willing to actually destroy it in the process. In other words, the first principles are lost, and one is caught up in the frenzy of attack and defense.

What becomes clear very soon is that Morin's quest for complex thought is not merely some dry logical exercise. It is all about the way we organize our experience, how we make meaning of the world, how we live our lives, and how we can choose between lives that aspire to wisdom and compassion and the dangers of disjunctive, demonizing terror. And in the process, imagination and emotions play an absolutely crucial role, as Morin explores in detail in works like *L'identité humaine* (Morin, 2003). Much of the impetus behind simple thought is the emotions evoked by the perception of threat, the need for clarity, the assumption that anything other than a "strong stance," a powerful "position," is wishy-washy and reflects weakness and a willingness to "give in" to the aggressor. There is a whole sociology and psychology of knowledge at play here, which Morin has masterfully discussed in *Method*, particularly Volumes 3 and 4 (Morin, 1986, 1991).

Particularly relevant here is the introduction of the knower into the process of inquiry. The tradition of reductive, dualistic thought eliminates the knower from the process of knowing. With Morin we find the knower taking center stage and becoming a subject of inquiry, self-reflection and self-analysis (Morin, 1971). This opens up an entirely different understanding of the nature of inquiry, deepening the complexity and forcing the inquirer to take responsibility for his or her own process. Not unlike the process of training required for psychoanalysts, Morinian inquiry involves a recognition that all inquiry is engaged by a human being, not an objective lens with no emotions, stressors, political and social constraints, and so on. Inquiry therefore requires a process of self-inquiry.

Morin's introduction of the knower is not a fall into "absolute" subjectivism—far from it. It is rather a call for a discipline of thinking, inquiry, and being. If knowing is always performed by somebody, then that somebody can be viewed as an instrument, an instrument that has to be tuned, studied, practiced. Limitations and blind spots have to be assessed and brought into consciousness.

In an age of fundamentalisms and black and white, dualistic thinking, Morin's work is more timely than ever. In his political works he has applied complex thought to the nature of the USSR, the future of Europe, and the conflict in the Middle East. In these works, Morin outlines a complex perspective on these issues that provides us with an alternative to the simple thought of both fundamentalist and liberal thinkers. Morin's oeuvre opens up a world of possibilities and presents us with the tools to address the enormous complexity of today's world. Morin challenges us to explore the meaning of inquiry—and show us how this seemingly esoteric question lies at the heart of the challenge for the 21st century. One can only hope that his Method will be widely studied and applied to address our global challenges and prepare us to do this with creativity, wisdom, and compassion.

Alfonso Montuori
San Francisco, California, United States

REFERENCES

Adorno, T. W., Frenkel-Brunswik, E., Levinson, D. J., & Sanford, R. N. (1982). *The authoritarian personality* (Abridged ed.). New York: Norton.

Anselmo, A. (2005). *Edgar Morin e gli scienziati contemporanei* [Edgar Morin and contemporary scientists]. Soveria Mannelli: Rubbettino.

Anselmo, A. (2006). *Edgar Morin: Dalla sociologia all'epistemologia* [Edgar Morin: From sociology to epistemology]. Napoli: Guida.

Atlan, H. (1986). *A Tort et à Raison. Intercritique de la Science et du Mythe*. Paris: Seuil.

Bachelard, G. (2002). *The formation of the scientific spirit*. Manchester: Clinamen Press.

Barron, F. (1995). *No rootless flower: Towards an ecology of creativity*. Cresskill, NJ: Hampton Press.

Bateson, G. (2002). *Mind and nature: A necessary unity*. Cresskill, NJ: Hampton Press.

Benkirane, R. (2006). *La complexité, vertiges et promesses. 18 histoires de sciences. Entretiens avec Edgar Morin, Ilya Prigogine, Francisco Varela . . .* [Complexity, giddiness and promises. 18 stories of science. Dialogues with Edgar Morin, Ilya Prigogine, Francisco Varela . . .]. Paris: Le Pommier.

Bernstein, R. (2005). *The abuse of evil: Politics and religion after 9/11*. Malden. MA: Polity Press.

Bianchi, F. (2001). *Le fil des idées. Une éco-biographie intellectuelle d'Edgar Morin* [The thread of ideas. An intellectual eco-biography of Edgar Morin]. Paris: Seuil.

Bocchi, G., & Ceruti, M. (2002). *The narrative universe*. Cresskill, NJ: Hampton Press.

Boorstin, D. J. (1992). *The image: A guide to pseudo-events in America*. New York: Vintage.

Bougnoux, D., Le Moigne, J.-L., & Proulx, S. (Eds.). (1990). *Arguments pour une méthode* [Arguments for a method]. Paris: Editions du Seuil.

Byers, W. (2007). *How mathematicians think: Using ambiguity, contradiction, and paradox to create mathematics*. Princeton, NJ: Princeton University Press.

Capra, F. (1996). *The web of life*. New York: Anchor.

Cassé, M., & Morin, E. (2003). *Enfants du ciel. Entre vide, lumière, matiére* [Children of the sky. Between the void, light, and matter]. Paris: Odile Jacob.

Ceruti, M. (2008). *Evolution without foundation*. Cresskill, NJ: Hampton Press.

Chambers, I. (1993). Cities without maps. In J. Bird (Ed.), *Mapping the futures: Local cultures global change* (pp. 188-197). New York: Routledge.

Chambers, I. (1994). *Migrancy, culture, identity*. New York: Routledge.

Code, L. (1991). *What can she know? Feminist theory and the construction of knowledge*. Ithaca, NY: Cornell University Press.

Collins, R. (1998). *The sociology of philosophies: A global history of intellectual change*. Cambridge: MA: Belknap Harvard.

Coser, L. (1997). *Men of ideas*. New York: Pocket.

Davies, P. (1989). *The cosmic blueprint. New discoveries in the nature's creative ability to order the universe*. New York: Simon and Schuster.

Descartes, R. (1954). *Philosophical writings*. London: Open University.

de Saint Cheron, M. (2000). *De la memorie a la responsabilité. Dialogues avec Geneviéve de Gaulle Anhonioz, Edgar Morin, Emmanuel Levinas* [From memory to responsibility. Dialogues with Geneviéve de Gaulle Anhonioz, Edgar Morin, Emmanuel Levinas]. Paris: Éditions DERVY.

de Vallombreuse, P., & Morin, E. (2006). *Peuples*. [Peoples]. Paris: Flammarion.

Dortier, J.-F. (2006). Edgar Morin. Le paradigme perdu: La nature humaine [Edgar Morin. The lost paradigm: Human nature]. In M. Fournier (Ed.), *La bibliotheque idéale des sciences humaines* [The ideal library of the human sciences]. Auxerre cedex: Éditions Sciences Humaines.

Drake, D. (2002). *Intellectuals and politics in post-war France*. New York: Palgrave Macmillan.

Eliade, M. (1978). *Occultism, witchcraft, and cultural fashions: Essays in comparative religions*. Chicago: University of Chicago Press.

Fages, J. B. (1980). *Comprendre Edgar Morin* [Understanding Edgar Morin]. Toulouse: Privat.

Fay, B. (1996). *Contemporary philosophy of social science*. New York: Blackwell Publishers.

Fortin, R. (2002). *Comprendre la complexite. introduction a la methode d'Edgar Morin* [Understanding complexity. Introduction to Edgar Morin's Method]. Paris: L'Harmattan.

Green, A. (2005). *Key ideas for a contemporary psychoanalysis: Misrecognition and recognition of the unconscious*. New York: Routledge.

Guidano, V. F. (1987). *Complexity of the self. A developmental approach to psychopathology and therapy*. New York: Guilford.

Holton, G. (1988). *Thematic origins of scientific thought. Kepler to Einstein*. Cambridge, MA: Harvard University Press.

Journet, N. (2000). Qu'est-ce que la postmodernité? In J.-F. Dortier (Ed.), *Philosophies de notre temps* [Philosophies of our times] (pp. 113-120). Auxerre: Editions Sciences Humaines.

Jung, C. G. (1976). *The portable Jung*. New York: Penguin.

Kegan, R. (1982). *The evolving self*. Cambridge, MA: Harvard University Press.

Kegan, R. (1998). *In over our heads: The mental demands of modern life*. Boston: Harvard University Press.

Kofman, M. (1996). *Edgar Morin. From Big Brother to fraternity*. London: Pluto Press.

Kristeva, J. (1997). *The portable Kristeva*. New York: Columbia University Press.

Le Sueur, J. D., (2003). Decolonizing "French Universalism": Reconsidering the impact of the Algerian war on French intellectuals. In J. D. Le Sueur (Ed.), *The decolonization reader* (pp. 103-118). New York: Routledge.

Lechte, J. (1994). *50 key thinkers*. New York: Routledge.

Lyotard, J.-F. (1984). *The postmodern condition: A report on knowledge*. Manchester: Manchester University Press.

Maturana, H., & Varela, F. (1987). *The tree of knowledge*. Boston: New Science Library.

Montuori, A. (2005a). Gregory Bateson and the challenge of transdisciplinarity. *Cybernetics and Human Knowing, 12*(1-2), 147-158.

Montuori, A. (2005b). How to make enemies and influence people. Anatomy of totalitarian thinking. *Futures, 37*, 18-38.

Montuori, A. (2006). The quest for a new education: From oppositional identities to creative inquiry. *ReVision, 28*(3), 4-20.

Montuori, A., & Purser, R. (1999). *Social creativity* (Vol. 1). Cresskill, NJ: Hampton Press.

Morin, E. (1970). *The red and the white*. New York: Pantheon Books.

Morin, E. (1971). *Rumor in Orleans*. New York: Blond.

Morin, E. (1974). *L'homme et la mort*. [Humanity & Death] Paris: Seuil.

Morin, E. (1979). *Le paradigme perdu* [The lost paradigm]. Paris: Seuil (Originally published 1973)

Morin, E. (1981). *La méthode. 1. La nature de la nature* [Method. 1. The nature of nature]. Paris: Seuil.

Morin, E. (1982). *Le vif du sujet*. Paris: Seuil (Originally published 1969)

Morin, E. (1983). Beyond determinism: The dialogue of order and disorder. *SubStance, 40*, 22-35.

Morin, E. (1985). *La Méthode, tome 2. La vie de la vie* [Method, volume 2. The life of life]. Paris: Seuil.

Morin, E. (1986). *La conoscenza della conoscenza* [Knowledge of knowledge]. Milano: Feltrinelli.

Morin, E. (1990). *Science avec conscience* [Science with conscience]. Paris: Seuil.

Morin, E. (1991). *Le idee: Habitat, vita, organizzazione, usi e costumi* [Ideas: Habitat, life, organization, use, and customs]. Milano: Feltrinelli.

Morin, E. (1992a). *Method: Towards a study of humankind. The nature of nature*. New York: Peter Lang.

Morin, E. (1992b). *Viaggio in Cina* [Voyage to China]. Bergamo: Moretti & Vitali.

Morin, E. (1993). For a crisiology. *Industrial & Environmental Crisis Quarterly, 7*, 5-22.

Morin, E. (1994a). *Journal d'un livre/juillet 1980-aout 1981* [Diary of a book/July 1980-August 1981]. Paris: Interéditions.

Morin, E. (1994b). *La complexité humaine* [Human complexity]. Paris: Flammarion.

Morin, E. (1994c). *Sociologie* [Sociology]. Paris: Seuil.

Morin, E. (1996). *Vidal et le siens* [Vidal and his people]. Paris: Seuil.

Morin, E. (1999a). *Introduction à une politique de l'homme* [Introduction to a human politics]. Paris: Seuil (Originally published 1965)

Morin, E. (Ed.). (1999b). *Relier les conaissances: Le défi du XXIe siècle* [Reconnecting knowledge: The challenge of the 21st century]. Paris: Seuil.

Morin, E. (2000, February). Pardonner, c'est resister à la cruauté du monde [Forgiving is resisting the world's cruelty]. *Le Monde des Débats*.

Morin, E. (2001a). *Journal de Plozevet*. Paris: Editions de l'Aube.

Morin, E. (2001b). *Seven complex lessons in education for the future*. Paris: UNESCO.

Morin, E. (2003). *La Méthode, l'humanité de l'humanité, tome 5: L'Identité humaine* [Method, humanity of humanity, volume 5. Human identity]. Paris: Seuil.

Morin, E. (2004a). *Autocritique* [Self-criticism]. Paris: Seuil (Originally published 1959)

Morin, E. (2004b). *Pour entrer dans le XXIe siècle* [Entering the 21st century]. Paris: Seuil.

Morin, E. (2005a). *The stars*. Minneapolis: University of Minnesota Press.

Morin, E. (2005b). *The cinema, or the imaginary man*. Minneapolis: University of Minnesota Press.

Morin, E. (2005c). Re: From prefix to paradigm. *World Futures: The Journal of General Evolution, 61*, 254-267.

Morin, E. (2006a). *La Méthode, time 6. Ethique* [Method, volume 6. Ethics]. Paris: Seuil.

Morin, E. (2006b). *Le monde moderne et la question juive* [The modern world and the Jewish question]. Paris: Seuil.

Morin, E. (2007). Restricted complexity, general complexity. In C. Gershenson, D. Aerts, & B. Edmonds (Eds.), *Worldviews, science, and us: Philosophy and complexity*. New York: World Scientific Publishing Company.

Morin, E. (2008). *On complexity*. Cresskill, NJ: Hampton Press.

Morin, E., & Appel, K. (1984). *New York*. Paris: Galilée.

Morin, E., & Hulot, E. (2007). *L'an I de l'ère écologique, et dialogue avec Nicolas Hulot* [Year 1 of the ecological era and dialogue with Nicolas Hulot]. Paris: Tallandier.

Morin, E., & Kern, B. (1999). *Homeland earth: A manifesto for the new millennium*. Cresskill, NJ: Hampton Press.

Morin, E., & Le Moigne, J.-L. (1999). *L'intelligence de la complexité* [The intelligence of complexity]. Paris: L'Harmattan.

Morin, E., Lefort, C., & Castoriadis, C. (1968). *Mai 1968: la brèche: premières réflexions sur les événements* [May 1968: The breach: First reflections on the events]. Paris: Fayard.

Morin, E., & Nair, S. (1997). *Une politique de civilisation* [A politics of civilization]. Paris: Arléa.

Morin, E., & Piattelli Palmarini, M. (Eds.). (1978). *L'unité de l'homme* [Human unity] (Vol. 1-3). Paris: Seuil.

Mortimer, L. (2001). We are the dance: Cinema, death, and the imaginary in the thoughts of Edgar Morin. *Thesis Eleven, 64*, 77-95.

Nicolescu, B. (1997). Levels of complexity and levels of reality: Nature as trans-nature. In B. Pullman (Ed.), *The emergence of complexity in mathematics, physics, chemistry, and biology* (pp. 393-410). Princeton: Princeton University Press.

Nicolescu, B. (2002). *Manifesto of transdisciplinarity*. Albany: SUNY Press.

Paz, O. (1986). *One earth, four or five worlds: Reflections on contemporary history*. New York: Harvest/HBJ.

Purser, R.E., & Montuori, A. (Eds.). (1999). *Social creativity* (Vol. 2). Cresskill, NJ: Hampton Press.

Rosetto Ajello, A. (2003). *Il rigore e la scommessa. Riflessioni sociopedagogiche sul pensiero di Edgar Morin* [Rigor and wager. Sociopedagogical reflections on Edgar Morin's thought]. Caltanissetta: Sciascia.

Rouch, J. & Morin, E. (Directors) (2005). *Chronique d'un été* [DVD]. Paris: G.C.T.H.V.

Roux-Rouquié, M. (2002). *Le concept de vie chez Edgar Morin. Une biologie pur le XXIe siècle* [Morin's concept of life. A biology for the 21st century]. Paper presented at the 3° Conférence d'Epistémologie et de Philosophie. http://www.mcxapc.org/docs/ateliers/rouquie.htm.

Selvini Palazzoli, M. (1990). *The hidden games of organizations*. New York: Routledge.

Spire, A. (1999). *La pensée Prigogine suivi de trois entretiens avec Gilles Cohen-Tannoudji, Daniel Bensaid, Edgar Morin* [Prigogine thought, followed by three dialogues with Gilles Cohen-Tannoudji, Daniel Bensaid, Edgar Morin]. Paris: Desclée de Brouwer.

Sorokin, P.A. (1964). *The Basic Trends of Our Times*. New Haven, CT: College and University Press.

Taylor, M. (2003). *The moment of complexity. Emerging network culture*. Chicago: University of Chicago Press.

Toffler, A. (1984). *Future shock*. New York: Bantam.

Touraine, A. (2001). Le complex l'homme et l'oeuvre. [The complex man and work]. In G. Lopez Ospina & N. Vallejo-Gomez (Eds.), *L'humaniste planetaire. L'humaniste planetaire. Edgar Morin en ses 80 ans—Hommage international* [The planetary humanist. Edgar Morin at 80—An international homage] (pp. 278-283). Quito: UNESCO.

Ungar, S. (2003). The thick of things: Rouch and Morin's Chronique d'une été reconsidered. *French Cultural Studies, 14*(5), 5-22.

Veloso, C. (2003). *Tropical truth: A story of music and revolution in Brazil*. New York: Da Capo Press.

Watzlawick, P. (1977). *How real is real?* New York: Vintage.

Westbroek, P. (2004). Gaia, Ockham's razor and the science of complexity. *World Futures: The Journal of General Evolution, 60*(5-6), 407-420.

Wilshire, B. (1990). *The moral collapse of the university: Professionalism, purity, and alienation*. Albany: SUNY Press.

Winston, B. (1995). *Claiming the real. The documentary film revisited*. London: British Film Institute.

Yassine, A. (2000). *Winning the modern world for Islam*. New Britain, PA: Justice and Spirituality Publishing.

Young, T. (2002, November 30). Twilight of the idols. *The Spectator*.

1

BLIND
INTELLIGENCE

BECOMING AWARE

We have acquired extraordinary knowledge about the physical, biological, psychological, and sociological world. Science is increasingly expanding the domain of empirical and logical methods of verification. The "light" of Reason seems to have driven myths and "darkness" to the dregs of the human spirit. At the same time, everywhere, error, ignorance, and blindness advance alongside our knowledge.

A radical awareness is required:

1. The deep cause of error is not error of fact (false perception), or error of logic (incoherence), but rather the way we organize our knowledge into a system of ideas (theories, ideologies);
2. There is a new ignorance related to the development of science itself;
3. There is a new blindness about the deteriorated use of reason;
4. The most serious threats that humanity faces are the blind and uncontrollable advances of knowledge (thermonuclear weapons, manipulations of all sorts, ecological imbalances, etc.)

I would like to demonstrate that these errors, ignorances, blindnesses, and dangers have a common characteristic that results in a mutilating way of organizing knowledge, an organization that is incapable of recognizing and apprehending the complexity of reality.

The Problem of the Organization of Knowledge

All knowledge operates through the selection of meaningful data and the rejection of data that are not meaningful. It does so by separating (distinguishing or disjointing) and unifying (associating, identifying), and by organizing into hierarchies (the primary, the secondary) and centralizing (around a core of master notions). These operations, which use logic, are in reality driven by "supralogical" principles of organization of thought, or paradigms: the hidden principles that govern our perception of things and of the world, without our being conscious of them.

Therefore, during the vague transition from a geocentric (Ptolemaic) to a heliocentric (Copernican) view of the world, the first contrast between the two worldviews was in the principle determining the selection and rejection of data. The supporters of the geocentric view rejected as meaningless all data that was inexplicable according to their worldview. The supporters of the other view used the same data as a foundation for conceptualizing the heliocentric system. The new system is made up of the same elements (the planets), and often uses the same calculations, but the entire worldview has changed. The rearranging of the Earth and Sun was much more than a simple permutation. It was rather a transformation of the center (the Earth) into a peripheral element, and of a peripheral element (the Sun) into the center.

Let us now take an example that is at the heart of the anthropo-social problems of our century: the concentration camp system (the Gulag) in the former Soviet Union. Even when acknowledged, de facto, it was possible to cast the Gulag out to the periphery of Soviet socialism, as a negative but secondary and temporary phenomenon, provoked primarily by an encroaching capitalism and the initial difficulties in the construction of socialism. But the Gulag could also be considered as the central core of the system, revealing its totalitarian essence. We see then how, depending on a logical operation—centration, organization into a hierarchy, disjunction or identification—our view of the USSR changes completely.

This example demonstrates how difficult it is to think of a phenomenon like "the nature of the USSR." Not because our prejudices, our passions, and our interests are at work behind the ideas, but because we do not have a means to conceive of the complexity of the problem. The issue is avoiding identification a priori (which reduces the notion of USSR to that of the Gulag) as well as a priori disjunction that dissociates the two, making the notion of socialism and the notion of concentration camps foreign to one another. It is avoiding the abstract, one-dimensional view. To do that, it is essential to first become aware of the nature and the consequences of paradigms that mutilate knowledge and disfigure reality.

THE PATHOLOGY OF KNOWING, BLIND INTELLIGENCE

We are dominated by the principles of disjunction, reduction, and abstraction. Together, they constitute what I call the "paradigm of simplification." Descartes formulated this master paradigm of Western civilization by disjoining the thinking subject (ego cogitans) and the thing being thought of (res extensa)—in other words, philosophy and science—and by positing "clear and distinct" ideas as principles of reality—in other words, disjunctive thought itself. This paradigm has dominated the adventure of Western thought since the seventeenth century. It has without doubt allowed for very great progress in scientific knowledge and in philosophical reflection. Its ultimately noxious consequences did not begin to become clear until the twentieth century.

This kind of disjunction reduced communication between scientific knowledge and philosophical reflection to a trickle. It eventually deprived science of any possibility of knowing itself, of self-reflection, and even of conceiving of itself scientifically. What is more, the principle of disjunction radically isolated the three main branches of scientific knowledge from each other: physics, biology, and the human sciences.

The only way to remedy this disjunction was another simplification: the reduction of complexity to simplicity (reduction of the biological to the physical, of the human to the biological). Hyper-specialization tore up and fragmented the complex fabric of reality, and led to the belief that the fragmentation inflicted on reality was reality in itself. At the same time, the ideal of classical scientific knowledge was to discover, behind the apparent complexity of phenomena, a perfect Order, regulating a perpetual machine (the cosmos), which was in turn made up of micro-elements (atoms) diversely assembled into objects and systems.

This knowledge necessarily built its rigor on, and was operationalized by, measurement and calculation. But mathematization and formalization increasingly disintegrated beings and things. They only considered as real the formulas and equations governing quantified entities. In short, simple thought is incapable of conceiving the conjunction of the one and the many (unitas multiplex). Simple thought unifies abstractly, canceling out diversity. Or, on the contrary, it posits diversity without conceiving of unity.

In this way, we arrive at blind intelligence. Blind intelligence destroys unities and totalities. It isolates all objects from their environment. It cannot conceive of the inseparable link between the observer and the observed. Key realities are disintegrated. They slip through the cracks between disciplines. The disciplines of the human sciences no longer need the concept of the "human." Blind pedants conclude that "man" does not exist, that it is only an illusion. Whereas the media produces mass ignorance, the university produces high ignorance. The dominant methodology produces an increasing obscurantism: because there are no longer any links between the disjointed elements of knowledge, so there is no longer an opportunity to truly absorb them and reflect on them.

We are approaching an unprecedented mutation of knowledge. Knowledge is less and less made to be reflected upon and discussed by human minds, and it is more and more made to be imprinted in memory banks and manipulated by anonymous powers, particularly by nation states. This new, massive, and prodigious ignorance is itself ignored by scientists. Scientists who do not practically master the consequences of their discoveries, do not control the meaning and nature of their research even on an intellectual level.

Human problems are handed over not just to this scientific obscurantism that produces ignorant specialists, but also to obtuse doctrines that attempt to monopolize the scientific, confining it to a single key idea (Althusserian

Marxism, liberal econocracy). These ideas are all the poorer because they pretend to open all doors (with key concepts like desire, mimesis, disorder, etc.) as if truth were locked in a vault, and it were sufficient to have the key. At the same time, an ungrounded essayism further shares the stage with narrow-minded scientism.

Unfortunately, this mutilating, one-dimensional vision is taking a cruel toll on human phenomena. The mutilation wounds flesh, spills blood, spreads suffering. The inability to conceive of the complexity of anthroposocial reality, both in its micro dimension (the individual being), and in its macro dimension (the planetary collectivity of humanity), has led us to infinite tragedies and is leading us to the supreme tragedy. We are told that politics "must" be simple and Manichean. Yes, certainly, in its manipulative conception that thrives on blind impulses, but political strategy requires complex knowing, because strategy plays itself out by working with and against uncertainty, chance, the multiple play of interactions and retroactions (feedback loops).

THE NEED FOR COMPLEX THOUGHT

What is complexity? At first glance, complexity is a fabric (complexus: that which is woven together) of heterogeneous constituents that are inseparably associated: complexity poses the paradox of the one and the many. Next, complexity is in fact the fabric of events, actions, interactions, retroactions, determinations, and chance that constitute our phenomenal world. But complexity presents itself with the disturbing traits of a mess, of the inextricable, of disorder, of ambiguity, of uncertainty. Hence the necessity for knowledge to put phenomena in order by repressing disorder, by pushing aside the uncertain. In other words, to select the elements of order and certainty, and to eliminate ambiguity, to clarify, distinguish, and hierarchize. But such operations, necessary for intelligibility, risk leading us to blindness if they eliminate other characteristics of the complexus. And in fact, as I have argued, they have made us blind.

However, complexity has come back to us, in the sciences, by the same means that chased it out. The development of physical science, which took it upon itself to reveal the impeccable order of the world, its absolute and perpetual determinism, its obedience to a singular Law and its constitution of a simple, primary matter (the atom), has finally opened up to the complexity of reality. We have discovered in the physical universe a hemorrhaging principle of degradation and disorder, the second principle of thermodynamics. So, in place of the supposed logical and physical simplicity, we discovered extreme microphysical complexity. Particles are not primary building blocks, but rather a frontier onto a perhaps inconceivable complexity. The cosmos is not a perfect machine, but a process of simultaneous organization and disorganization.

Finally, it appears that life is not a substance but a phenomenon of extraordinarily complex self-eco-organization that produces autonomy. From now on, it is evident that anthropo-social phenomena cannot obey principles of intelligibility that are less complex than those henceforth required for natural phenomena. We must face anthropo-social complexity, and not dissolve or dissimulate it.

The difficulty of complex thought is that it must face messes (the infinite play of inter-retroactions), interconnectedness among phenomena, fogginess, uncertainty, contradiction. However, we can elaborate some conceptual tools, some principles for this adventure, and we can begin to perceive the face of the new paradigm of complexity that should emerge.

I have already indicated in *La méthode*[1] some conceptual tools that we can use. So for the disjunction-reduction-unidimensionality paradigm, we can substitute a paradigm of distinction-conjunction that will allow us to distinguish without disjoining, to associate without identifying or reducing. This paradigm would include a dialogical and translogical principle that would integrate classical logic while taking into account its de facto limitations (problems of contradiction) and its de jure limitations (limitations of formalism). It would incorporate the principle of Unitas Multiplex, that escapes abstract unity whether high (holism) or low (reductionism).

My intention is not to enumerate the "commandments" of complex thought, which I have attempted to draw out elsewhere.[2] It is, rather, to recognize the enormous deficiencies in our thinking, and to understand that mutilating thought necessarily leads to mutilating actions. My intention is to increase awareness of the contemporary pathology of thought.

The ancient pathology of thought gave independent life to the myths and the gods that thought created. The modern pathology of mind is in the hypersimplification that makes us blind to the complexity of reality. The pathology of ideas takes the form of idealism, where the idea obscures the reality it is supposed to translate, and takes itself alone as real. The pathology of theory is in doctrinarism and dogmatism, which turn the theory in on itself and petrify it. The pathology of reason is rationalization, which encloses reality in a system of ideas that are coherent but partial and unilateral, and do not know that a part of reality is unrationalizable, and that rationality's mission is to dialogue with the unrationalizable.

We are blind to the problem of complexity. Epistemological disputes between Popper, Kuhn, Lakatos, Feyerabend, and others pass into relative silence.[3] This blindness is part of our barbarism. It makes us realize that in the world of ideas, we are still in an age of barbarism. We are still in the prehistory of the human mind. Only complex thought will allow us to civilize our knowledge.

2

COMPLEX
PATTERN AND DESIGN

Human science has neither a foundation that grounds human phenomena in the natural universe, nor methods that can grasp the extreme complexity that distinguishes human phenomena from all other known natural phenomena. Its explanatory framework (or armor) is still that of the physics of the nineteenth century. Its implicit ideology is still that of Christianity and Western human-ism—the super-naturality of the human. My approach will be a movement on two fronts. They may appear divergent, even antagonistic, but in my mind they are inseparable. We must, certainly, reintegrate humans with nature and we must be able to distinguish humans from nature, thereby not reducing humans to nature. We must, consequently, at the same time, develop a theory, a logic, and an epistemology of complexity that will be appropriate to the knowledge of human beings. We are looking for the unification of science and a theory addressing the very high degree of human complexity. It is a principle with deep roots whose developments are increasingly diversifying and branching out more and more the higher we go. I situate myself, therefore, well outside the two antagonistic clans: one that destroys difference by reducing it to a simple unity, the other that obscures unity by only seeing differences. I see myself well outside both, but I am attempting to integrate the two truths. In other words, I am attempting to go beyond the either/or alternative.

The research I have undertaken has increasingly convinced me that such a "going beyond" must lead to a chain reaction, a reorganization of what we understand under the concept of science. To tell the truth, a fundamental change, a paradigmatic revolution, seems necessary and near.

The solidity of evidence has been threatened. The tranquility of ignorance has been shaken. Already ordinary either/or alternatives have lost their absolute character, and other alternatives are taking shape. What authority has obscured, ignored, and rejected, is coming out of the shadows: the pedestal of knowledge is cracking.

INDO–AMERICA

We are, in this sense, simultaneously more advanced and more backward than one might believe. We have discovered the first coasts of America, but we still believe that it is the Indies. The cracks and tears in our conception of the world have not only become enormous gaps, but through the gaps, as with the shell of a crustacean who is shedding, as with the split in a cocoon, we can perceive fragments not yet connected, the new skin still wrinkled and shriveled, the new face, the new form.

First of all, there were two breaches in the epistemological framework of classical science. The breach of microphysics revealed the interdependence of subject and object, the insertion of randomness into knowledge, the de-reification of the notion of matter, the eruption of logical contradiction in empirical description. The breach of macro-physics unites in a single entity the concepts of space and time that have until now been absolutely heterogeneous, and shattered our concepts when they were carried off faster than the speed of light. But these two breaches, we thought, were infinitely far from our world, one too small, the other too large. We didn't want to admit that the moorings of our conception of the world had been broken apart at both ends, that we were, in our "middle band," not so much on the firm ground of an island surrounded by an ocean, but rather on a flying carpet.

There is no more firm ground, no terra firma. "Matter" is no longer the massive elementary and simple reality to which we could reduce physis. Space and time are no longer absolute and independent entities. There is no longer any simple empirical base, not even a simple logical base (clear and distinct notions, non-ambivalent, non-contradictory, a strictly determined reality) to constitute the physical substrata. From this stems a consequence of capital importance: simplicity (the categories of classical physics that constituted the model of all science) is no longer the foundation of all things, but a passage, a moment between complexities, between microphysical complexity and macro-cosmo-physical complexity.

SYSTEMS THEORY

Systems theory and cybernetics intersect in a common, uncertain zone. In principle, the scope of systems theory is much wider, quasi-universal, because, in a certain sense, all known reality, from the molecule to the cell to an organism to a society, can be conceived of as systems. That is to say, they can be conceived as the interaction of different elements. In fact, systems theory, launched with von Bertalanffy from a reflection on biology, spread, from the 1950s, burgeoning in widely differing directions.

Systems theory offers an ambiguous face to the external observer. For the observer who would go beyond this ambiguous exterior, systems theory offers at least three faces, three contradictory directions. There is a generative systemism that carries a principle of complexity.[4] There is a vague, flat systemism, founded on the repetition of a few aseptic (holistic) primary truths that mean little in practice. And there is systems analysis, which is the systemic equivalent of cybernetic engineering, but much less reliable. It transforms systemism into its opposite, in other words, as the term analysis indicates, into reductive operations.

Systemism has, first of all, the same generative aspects of cybernetics, which in using the concept of the machine as reference, conserves in abstraction some of its concrete and empirical origins. The virtue of systemism is:

1. to have placed at the center of the theory, with the notion of system, not an elementary, discrete unity, but a complex unity, a whole that cannot be reduced to the sum of its constituent parts;
2. to have conceived the notion of system, not as a "real" notion, not as a purely formal notion, but as an ambiguous, ghostly notion;
3. to situate itself at a transdisciplinary level, which allows both the concept of the unity of science and the differentiation of the sciences, not only according to the material nature of their object, but also according to the types and complexities of associational and organizational phenomena. In this last sense, the scope of systems theory is not only wider than that of cybernetics, but its vastness extends to all that is knowable.

OPEN SYSTEMS

The concept of open system originated as a thermodynamic notion. Its primary characteristic was to allow the circumscription, in a negative way, of the application of the second principle. This principle requires the notion of a closed system, which does not itself dispose of an external source of matter/energy. This definition would be uninteresting except that one can now consider a certain number of physical systems (the flame of a candle, the flow of a river around the piling of a bridge), and especially living systems, as systems whose existence and structure depend on an external source. In the case of living systems, this means not only energy and matter, but also organizational and informational resources.

This means that:

1. a bridge is built between thermodynamics and the life sciences;
2. a new idea emerges in opposition to the physical notions of equilibrium/disequilibrium, and goes beyond one and the other, in a sense containing them both.

A closed system, like a rock or a table, is in a state of equilibrium. In other words, matter and energy exchanges with the exterior are nonexistent. The constancy of the flame of a candle, the constancy of the internal environment of a cell or an organism are not at all linked to such an equilibrium. There is, on the contrary, disequilibrium in the energetic flux that feeds them, and without this flux, there is an organizational deregulation that quickly leads to decline.

In a first sense, this nourishing disequilibrium allows the system to maintain an apparent equilibrium, a state of stability and continuity, in other words. This apparent equilibrium only degrades if left to itself, in other words, if there is a closure of the system. This guaranteed state, constant but fragile (the term we will use here is steady state), is somewhat paradoxical. The structures remain the same even though the constituents are changing. This is not only true for the whirlpool or the flame of a candle, but also of our organisms, where our molecules and cells are renewing themselves incessantly, while the whole remains apparently stable and stationary. In a way the system has to close itself off from the outside world to maintain its structures and its internal environment. If it did not, it would disintegrate. This closure is allowed by the very fact that the system is open.

The problem becomes even more interesting when we suppose an indissoluble relationship between maintaining the structure and its changing constituents. Here we find a primary, central, obviously key problem of living beings. This problem is, however, ignored and obscured, not only by the old physics, but also by Western Cartesian metaphysics, for whom all living things are considered closed entities, not as systems that organize their closing (that is to say, their autonomy) in and by their opening.

Two capital consequences flow from the idea of an open system: the first is that the laws of organization of the living are not laws of equilibrium, but rather of disequilibrium, recovered or compensated, stabilized dynamics. We will, in our work, follow these ideas closely. The second consequence, perhaps more important still, is that the intelligibility of the system has to be found, not only in the system itself, but also in its relationship with the environment, and that this relationship is not a simple dependence: it is constitutive of the system.

Reality is therefore as much in the connection (relationship) as in the distinction between the open system and its environment. This connection is absolutely crucial epistemologically, methodologically, theoretically, and empirically. Logically, the system cannot be understood except by including the environment. The environment is at the same time intimate and foreign: it is a part of the system while remaining exterior to it.

Methodologically, it becomes difficult to study open systems as entities that can be radically isolated. Theoretically and empirically, the concept of an open system opens the door to a theory of evolution, that can only come from the interaction of system and eco-system, and, in its most significant organizational leaps, can be conceived of as the "going beyond," the surpassing, of the system into a meta-system. The door is, therefore, open for a theory of self-eco-organizing systems. These systems are themselves open, of course, because far from escaping 'openness,' evolution toward complexity increases it. In other words, it is a theory of living systems.

Finally, because the fundamental relationship between open systems and the eco-system is of both a matter/energy and of an organizational/informational nature, we can attempt to understand the character, both deterministic and contingent, of the eco-systemic relationship.

It is extraordinary that an idea as fundamental as the open system emerged so late and so locally (which demonstrates already how the obvious is the most difficult to perceive). In fact, this notion is present but not explicitly engaged in some theories, notably in Freud's. The Ego is a system open onto the Id and the Superego. It can only constitute itself through them, and maintains ambiguous but fundamental relations with both. The idea of personality in cultural anthropology also implies that it is a system open to culture (but unfortunately in this discipline culture itself is a closed system.)

The concept of an open system has a paradigmatological value. As Maruyama (1974) has remarked, to conceive of all objects and entities as closed leads to a vision of the world that is classificatory, analytical, reductionist, with linear causality. This vision reigned supreme in physics from the seventeenth to the nineteenth century. Today, with the deepening understanding of, and advances toward, complexity, this vision is taking on water from all sides. We must, in fact, carry out an epistemological reversal, beginning with the notion of open system. "Those people who live in the classificatory universe proceed with the perception that all systems are closed, unless otherwise specified."[5] In my thinking, Gödel's theorem, in making an irreparable breach in all axiomatic systems, allows us to conceive of theory and logic as open systems.

Systems theory syncretically assembles the most diverse elements; in one sense, this creates an excellent petrie dish, in another, confusion. However, this favorable milieu has elicited contributions that are often fecund in their diversity.

In a way somewhat analogous to cybernetics, but in a different field, systems theory moves toward a middle range. On one end, it has barely explored the concept of system itself, and it is satisfied in this fundamental point by an all-purpose "holism." On the other end, it has hardly begun to explore the direction of self-organization and complexity. There remains an enormous conceptual void between the notion of an open system and the complexity of the most elementary living system, a void that is not satisfied by von Bertalanffy's theses on hierarchy.[6]

Finally, systems theory, because it responds to an increasingly pressing need, often makes its entrance into the human sciences from two unfortunate angles. One is technocratic[7] and the other all-purpose; too much general abstraction breaks away from the concrete and does not succeed in forming a coherent model. However, let us not forget that here is the germ of the unity of science. Systemism must be assimilated if it is to be superseded.

INFORMATION/ORGANIZATION

We have already encountered the notion of information with cybernetics. We might have also encountered it with systems theory, but we must consider information not as an ingredient, but as a theory that demands preliminary, independent, examination.

Information is a central yet problematic notion. From this stems all its ambiguity: we can say very little about it, but we can't do without it.

Information emerged with Hartley, and especially with Shannon and Weaver, as, on the one hand, communicational (we are speaking here of the transmission of messages as it is integrated in a theory of communication) and on the other hand, as an aspect of statistics (dealing with the probability or rather the improbability of the appearance of this or that elementary unit carrying information, or binary digit, bit). Its first field of application was the field in which it emerged—telecommunications.

Very soon, however, through the connection with cybernetics, the transmission of information became pertinent to organization. In fact, a "program" carrying information does not only communicate a message to a computer: it commands a certain number of operations.

More fascinating yet was the possibility of extrapolating the theory very heuristically to the biological domain. As soon as it was established that a cell's (or an organism's) self-reproduction could be conceived from a duplication of genetic material or DNA, as soon as it was conceived that DNA constituted a sort of double helix whose rungs were constituted of chemical quasi-signs of which the whole could constitute a hereditary quasi-message, then reproduction could be conceived of as a copy of a message. In other words, reproduction could be conceived of as an emission-reception covered by communication theory: it was possible to liken each chemical element to discrete units, empty of meaning (like phonemes or letters of the alphabet), combining into complex units, carriers of meaning (like words). Even more, genetic mutation was likened to "noise" disrupting the reproduction of a message, provoking an "error" (at least in respect to the original message) in the constitution of the new message. The same informational scheme could be applied to the functioning of the cell, where DNA constitutes a kind of "program" that orients and governs metabolic activities. In this way, the cell could be cyberneticized, and the key element of this cybernetic explanation could be found in information. Here again, a theory of communicational origin was applied to an organizational reality. And, in this application, it is necessary to consider organizational information as a memory, as a message, as a program, or rather, like all of them at once.

And further: if the notion of information could, on the one hand, be integrated into the notion of biological organization, it could, on the other hand, somewhat surprisingly link thermodynamics, or physics, to biology.

In effect, the second principle of thermodynamics was formulated by a probability equation that expressed the tendency toward entropy, in other words, toward increasing disorder over order at the heart of a system, of the disorganized over the organized. But, the Shannonian equation of information ($H=KlnP$) was like the mirror image, the negative, of the equation for entropy ($S=KlnP$) in the sense that entropy is inversely proportional to information. From here came the idea, clarified by Brillouin, that there is equivalence between information and negative entropy or negentropy. Here again we find the relationship between organization and information, with the addition of a theoretical foundation that allows us to understand the link and the rupture between physical order and living order.

Information is, therefore, a concept that establishes the link with physics, while at the same time being fundamentally unknown in physics. It is inseparable from biological organization and complexity. It brings into science the spiritual object that had only found a place in metaphysics. This is quite a crucial notion, a Gordian knot, but like the Gordian knot, it is intertwined and cannot be disentangled. Information is a problem concept, not a solution concept. It is an indispensable concept, but it is not yet an elucidated or elucidating concept.

Because, let us remember, what has emerged of information theory, the communicational aspect and the statistical aspect, are like a thin surface of an immense iceberg. The communicational aspect in no way takes into consideration the polyscopic character of information, which presents itself to our view as memory, as knowledge, as message, as program, as organizational matrix.

The statistical aspect ignores, even within the communicational framework, the meaning of the information. It doesn't seize anything other than the issue of probability-improbability. It does not consider the structure of messages and, of course, ignores the entire organizational aspect. The Shannonian theory finds itself at the level of entropy, of the degradation of information. It is situated in the framework of this fatal degradation, and it has allowed us to find ways to reduce the fatal effect of noise. In other words, current theory is not capable of understanding either the birth or the growth of information.

Therefore, the concept of information presents great gaps and great uncertainties. This is not a reason to reject it, but rather to deepen our understanding of it. There is in this concept an enormous richness, under the surface, that would like to take body and form. This is, obviously, at the opposite extreme to informational ideology, which reifies information, substantializes it, makes it into an entity of the same nature as matter and energy—in short it makes the concept regress on those positions that it is designed to go beyond. Information is not an end-of-the-line concept, but rather, a point-of-departure concept. It reveals to us a limited and superficial aspect of a phenomenon that is at the same time radical and polyscopic, inseparable from organization.

ORGANIZATION

As we have just seen, each in its own way, cybernetics, systems theory, information theory, in their simultaneous generativity and insufficiency, call for a theory of organization. In a parallel way, modern biology has passed from organicism to organizationalism. For Piaget, this has been done already: "We have finally come to conceive of the concept of organization as the central concept of biology."[8] However, François Jacob sees clearly that the "general theory of organizations" has not been elaborated and has yet to be built.

Organization, a decisive yet barely glimpsed notion, is not yet, dare I say it, an organized concept. This notion can be elaborated starting with a complexification and a concretization of systemism, and can then appear as a yet unachieved development of systems theory. It can also be decanted from "organicism" on condition that there is a process that renders apparent the organism's organization.

It is important to point out right away the difference of level between the organizationism that we think is necessary, and traditional organicism. Organicism is a syncretic, historic, confused, romantic concept. Its starting point is from an organism conceived as an organized, harmonious totality, even when it carries within it antagonism and death. From this starting point, organicism makes of the organism a model both of the macrocosm (the organicist concept of the universe) and of human society. Therefore, a whole sociological current in the last century wanted to find in society an analogue of the animal organism, by looking meticulously for equivalencies between biological and social life.

Organizationism, on the other hand, seeks not to discover phenomenal analogies, but to find the common principles of organization, the principles of evolution of these principles, the characteristics of their diversification. From there, and only from there, phenomenal analogies might eventually hold some meaning.

But as opposed as they are, organizationism and organicism have some common foundation. The new cybernetic awareness no longer recoils at analogy, and it is not because organicism is founded on analogy that it should disturb us. It is more because the analogy was flat and trivial, because there was no theoretical foundation in these analogies, that organicism should be critiqued.

As Judith Schlanger says in her remarkable work on organicism: "The meticulous equivalencies between biological life and social life, as drawn by Schäffle, Lilienfeld, Worms, and even Spencer, these term by term comparisons are not the medium (support) of the analogy, but rather the foam that rises to the top."[9] On the contrary, this medium is, as we have said, a confused but rich conception of the organic totality.

We have denounced the romanticism of this conception. Now we must correct ourselves. Romantic organicism, like the organicism of the Renaissance, as it is found in Chinese thought (Needham, 1977), has always held that an organism obeys a complex and rich organization, that it can't be reduced to linear laws, to simple principles, to clear and distinct ideas, to a mechanistic vision. Organicism's virtue is in the prescience that vital organization cannot be understood according to the same logic as that of the artificial machine, and that the logical originality of the organism emerges through the complementarity of terms that, according to classical logic, are antagonistic, repulsive, contradictory. Organicism, in a word, presupposes a complex and rich organization, but it does not propose it.

The organism is also a machine in the sense that the word *organism* signifies an organized totality, but it is a machine of a different type from artificial machines. The alternative to reductionism is not in a vital principle, except in a living organizational reality. We see here to what extent we are completely out of step compared to traditional either/or alternatives: machine/organism, vitalism/reductionism.

However, if we decide to make the notions of organization and organism complementary, if the first is not strictly reductive, analytic, mechanistic, if the second is not only a totality carrying a vital, unspeakable mystery, then we can approach the problem of the living, because it is clearly with life that the notion of organization takes on an organismic thickness, a romantic mystery. This is where the fundamental traits that do not exist in artificial machines appear. There is a new relation to entropy, in other words, an aptitude, even if only temporary, to create negentropy, from entropy itself, a logic that is much more complex and without a doubt different from any artificial machine. Finally, indissociably linked to these two traits is the phenomenon of self-organization.

SELF-ORGANIZATION

Living organization—that is, self-organization—is far beyond the current possibilities of comprehension of cybernetics, systems theory, information theory and, of course, structuralism. It is even beyond the concept of organization itself, as it appears at its most advanced point, in Piaget, where it nevertheless remains blind to the little recursive prefix "self" the importance of which, phenomenal as well as epistemological, is paramount.

It is elsewhere that the problem of self-organization emerges: first, in the theory of self-reproducing automata, and second, in an attempt at a metacybernetic theory of self-organizing systems. In the case of the first, it is the brilliant inquiries of von Neumann that set out the fundamental principles,[10] and in the case of the second, the fundamental principles were set out during the three meetings on self-organizing systems in 1959, 1960, and 1961, in audacious attempts at theoretical breakthroughs, notably by Ashby, von Foerster, Gottard Gunther and several others.

But the outcome of the theory of self-organizing systems was doubly unfortunate compared to cybernetics. It was the application to artificial machines that made the fortune of cybernetics and atrophied its theoretical development. However, even though it is conceivable in principle to develop a theory of a self-organizing and self-reproducing artificial machine, the state of the theory and of technology at the time, and even today, made it impossible to conceive of creating such a machine. However, the theory of self-organization was made to understand the living, but it remained too abstract, too formal to deal with physico-chemical data and processes that make up the originality of living organization. Therefore, the theory of self-organization could not yet be applied to anything practical. Also, when funding ceased to feed the first theoretical efforts, the researchers, who all came from different disciplines, dispersed. Furthermore, the theory of self-organizing systems needed an epistemological revolution even more profound than that of cybernetics, and this need contributed to stopping its progress.

But there are points of departure, even if we can't truly speak of theory.

1. First of all, as early as 1945 Schrödinger outlined the paradox of living organization, which did not appear to obey the second thermodynamic principle.

2. Von Neumann situated the paradox in the difference between the living machine (self-organizing) and the artificial machine (simply organized). In fact, the artificial machine is constituted of very reliable elements (an engine, for example, is made of parts that have been double-checked and put together in the most durable and the most resistant way possible in light of the work function they are to fulfill). However, the machine, is, as a whole, much less reliable than each of its elements taken in isolation. In fact, it only takes a change in one of its constituent parts for the whole to be blocked, to break down, so that it can only be repaired by an external intervention (the mechanic). The living machine (self-organized), on the other hand, is entirely different. Its constituent parts are not very reliable. There are molecules that deteriorate very rapidly, and all organs are obviously made up of these molecules. Moreover, we see that in an organism, the molecules, as well as the cells, die and are renewed, to the point that the organism remains identical to itself even though all of its constituent parts have been renewed. There is, then, as opposed to the artificial machine, great reliability of the whole and weak reliability of the parts.

This shows not only the difference between the nature and logic of self-organizing systems and the others, but it also shows that there is a consubstantial link between disorganization and complex organization, because the phenomenon of disorganization (entropy) follows its course more rapidly in the living than in the artificial machine. In an inseparable way, there is the phenomenon of reorganization (negentropy). There lies the fundamental link between entropy and negentropy, in no way a Manichean opposition between two contrary entities. In other words, the link between life and death is much closer, much more profound, than we have been able to metaphysically imagine. Entropy, in a sense, contributes to the organization that it is destroying, and as we will see, self-organizing order cannot complexify itself but out of disorder; better yet, because we are in an informational order, out of noise (von Foerster, 1983).

This is a cornerstone of self-organization, and the paradoxical character of this proposition shows us that living order is not simple. It does not follow the logic that we apply to mechanical things, but postulates a logic of complexity.

3. The idea of self-organization creates a huge mutation in the ontological status of the object, one that goes beyond cybernetic ontology.

a. To start with, the object is phenomenologically individual. This constitutes a break with strictly physical objects given in nature. Physics and chemistry study, on one hand, the general laws that are followed by these objects, and on the other hand, their elementary units, molecules, atoms, which are, therefore, isolated from their phenomenal context (in other words, dissociated from the environment, which is always thought of as epiphenomenal). Phenomenal objects of a strictly physico-chemical universe do not have a principle of internal organization. However, for self-organizing objects, there is total equivalence between the phenomenal form and the principle of organization. This point, again, illustrates the radical differentiation between living and non-living. Certainly, the cybernetic object, in the case of an artificial machine, has an individuality linked to its organizing principle. But this principle is external, it is man-made. This is where the individuality of the living system distinguishes itself from that of other cybernetic systems.

b. In fact, it is endowed with autonomy. It is a relative autonomy, to be sure—and we need to remind ourselves of this constantly—but an organizational, organismic, and existential autonomy nevertheless. Self-organization is in fact a meta-

organization in relation to the orders of preexisting organization, and obviously, in relation to that of artificial machines.
This strange relation, this coincidence between the meta and
the self merits meditation.

Here, much more deeply than with cybernetics, we are drawn to grant the
object some of the privileges that have until now been reserved for the subject.
This also allows us to get a glimpse of how human subjectivity finds its sources,
its roots, in the world we call "objective."

But, at the same time that the self-organizing system detaches itself from
the environment and distinguishes itself, by its autonomy and its individuality,
it links itself ever more to the environment by increasing its openness and the
exchange that accompanies all progress of complexity: it is self-eco-organizing.
Although a closed system has little individuality and no exchanges with the
environment, the self-eco-organizing system has its individuality, linked to very
rich, and, therefore, dependent, relations with the environment. It is more
autonomous, and is less isolated. It needs supplies, matter/energy, but it also
needs information, order (Schrödinger). The environment is suddenly inside it,
and, as we will see, it plays a co-organizing role. The self-eco-organizing system, therefore, cannot suffice unto itself, it can't be totally logical except by
introducing, into itself, the foreign environment. It can't achieve itself, complete
itself, be self-sufficient.

COMPLEXITY

The idea of complexity has, until recently, had much more widespread popular
than scientific use. It always carried with it a warning to our understanding, a
cautioning against clarification, simplification, an overly rapid reduction. In
fact, complexity had its sacred ground, but without the actual word itself, in
philosophy; in a certain sense, its domain was dialectic, and in logic, Hegelian
dialectic, because Hegelian dialectic introduced contradiction and transformation at the heart of identity.

In twentieth century science, however, complexity had sprung up without
actually being called that, in micro-physics and macro-physics. Micro-physics
opened up not only onto a complex relationship between observer and
observed but also onto the more complex notion, the destabilizing notion, that
elementary particles appear to an observer as a wave, but also as a particle. But
micro-physics was considered as a borderline case, a frontier, and we forgot that
this frontier in fact concerned all material phenomena, including our own bodies and our own brains. Macro-physics, on the other hand, made observation
dependent on the position of the observer and complexified the relations

between time and space, until then considered transcendent and independent essences.

However these two complexities, micro- and macro-physics, were cast out to the periphery of our universe, even though they are about the foundations of our physis and they are characteristics of our cosmos. Between the two, in the physical, biological, and human domains, science reduced phenomenal complexity to simple order and elementary units. This simplification, let us repeat it, nourished the growth of Western science from the seventeenth to the end of the nineteenth century. Statistics, in the nineteenth century and the beginning of the twentieth century, allowed the treatment of interaction and interference.[11] There were attempts to refine, to work covariance and multi-variance, but these attempts were always insufficient, and always in the same reductionist perspective that ignores the reality of the abstract system from which the elements under consideration come.

It is with Wiener and Ashby, the founders of cybernetics, that complexity makes an entrance in the sciences. It is with von Neumann that, for the first time, the fundamental character of the concept of complexity appears in its relationship to the phenomena of self-organization.

What is complexity? At first glance, it is a quantitative phenomenon, the extreme quantity of interactions and of interference between a very large number of units. In fact, any (living) self-organizing system, even the simplest, combines a very large number of units, in the order of billions, whether molecules in a cell, or cells in an organism (more than 10 billion cells in the human brain, more than 30 billion for the organism).

But complexity is not only quantities of units and interactions that defy our possibilities of calculation; it also is made up of uncertainty, indetermination, and random phenomena. Complexity is, in a sense, always about chance.

Therefore, complexity coincides with a part of uncertainty that arises from the limits of our ability to comprehend, or with a part of uncertainty inscribed in phenomena. But complexity cannot be reduced to uncertainty; it is uncertainty at the heart of richly organized systems. It concerns semi-random systems in which the order is inseparable from the randomness that characterize them. Complexity is, therefore, linked to a certain mixture of order and disorder, a very intimate mixture, one that is very different from static conceptions of order/disorder, where order (impoverished and static) reigns at the level of large populations and disorder (impoverished because it is pure indetermination) reigns at the level of elementary units.

When cybernetics recognized complexity, it was to get around it, to put it in parentheses, but without denying it. It is the principle of the black box: one considers the inputs and the outputs. This allows one to study the results of the system's functioning, the resources needed by the system, the relationship between inputs and outputs, without ever entering into the mystery of the black box.

However, the theoretical problem of complexity concerns the possibility of getting inside black boxes. It is to consider organizational and logical complexity. Here, the difficulty is not only in the renewal of the concept of the object, it is in the reversal of the epistemological perspectives of the subject, in other words, of the scientific observer. The distinctive quality of science up to the present was to eliminate imprecision, ambiguity, contradiction. But an indubitable, inescapable imprecision must be accepted, not only in phenomena, but also in concepts, and one of the great advances in mathematics today is to consider fuzzy sets, imprecise wholes.[12]

One of the preliminary accomplishments in the study of the human brain is the understanding that one of the ways that it is superior to computers is its ability to work with the insufficient and the fuzzy. One must then accept an indubitable and inescapable ambiguity in the relations between subject/object, order/disorder, self-hetero-organization. One has to recognize phenomena, such as freedom or creativity, which are inexplicable outside the complex frame that allows their appearance.

Von Neumann pointed to the logical door of complexity. We will attempt to open it, but we don't hold the keys to the kingdom, and that is where our voyage remains unfinished. We will glimpse at this logic, starting with some of its external characteristics, we will define a few of its traits as yet unknown, but we will not be able to elaborate a new logic, not knowing if it is temporarily, or forever, out of our reach. But what we are persuaded of is that if our current logico-mathematical apparatus corresponds to certain aspects of phenomenal reality, it does not correspond to its truly complex aspects. That means that our logic has to develop itself, and go beyond itself in the direction of complexity. It is here that, in spite of his deep sense of the logic of biological organization, Piaget stopped at the edge of the Rubicon and sought only to accommodate living organization (reduced essentially to regulation), at the previously established logico-mathematic formalization.

Our only ambition will be to cross the Rubicon and venture into the new territories of complexity. We will attempt to go, not from the simple to the complex, but from complexity to ever increasing complexity. Let us repeat: the simple is no more than a moment, an aspect among several complexities (micro-physical, macro-physical, biological, psychic, social). We will attempt to consider the lines, the tendencies of a growing complexification, which will permit us, roughly, to determine models of low complexity, medium complexity, and high complexity as they function in the developments of self-organization (autonomy, individuality, richness of relations with the environment, aptitudes for learning, inventiveness, creativity, etc.). But, in the end, we will succeed in considering, with the human brain, truly amazing phenomena at a very high level of complexity, and to posit a new and capital notion for understanding the human problem—*hyper-complexity*.

SUBJECT AND OBJECT

Therefore, with the theories of self-organization and complexity, we touch on substrata shared by biology and anthropology, but beyond all biologism and anthropologism. They allow us to situate different levels of complexity where living beings are found, including the level of very high complexity, and sometimes hyper-complexity, characteristic of the anthropological phenomenon.

Such a theory allows us to reveal the relation between the physical universe and the biological universe, and ensures communication between all parts of what we call reality. Notions of physics and biology must not be reified. The borders on the map don't exist in the territory, but on the territory, with barbed wires and customs agents. If the concept of physics widens, becomes more complex, then everything is physics. I say that, therefore, biology, sociology, anthropology are specific branches of physics; in the same way, if biology widens, becomes more complex, then, everything that is sociological and anthropological is biological. Physics and biology alike cease to be reductionistic, simplifying, and they become fundamental. This is nearly incomprehensible if we are in the disciplinary paradigm where physics, biology, anthropology are distinct things, separate, noncommunicating.

In these pages, we will endeavor to elaborate about creating a theoretical opening, an open theory. Already, the reader can see that it permits emergence, in its own field, of what has been, up until now, cast out of science: the world and the subject.

The notion of open system, in fact, opens not only onto physics mediated by thermodynamics but, more broadly and profoundly, onto *physis*. In other words, it opens onto the orderly/disorderly nature of matter, onto an ambiguous, physical evolution that tends at the same time toward disorder (entropy) and organization (constitution of more and more complex systems). At the same time, the notion of an open system calls to mind the notion of environment. There we find not only physis as foundational material, but the world as a more vast horizon of reality, and beyond, opening up to infinity (because every eco-system can become an open system in another, vaster, eco-system, etc.). And so, from extension to extension, the notion of eco-system spreads out in all directions, all horizons.

The subject emerges with the emergence of the world. It emerges right at the start of cybernetics and systems perspective, there where a number of traits that are characteristic of human subjects (finality, program, communication, etc.) are included in the machine-object. It emerges particularly from self-organization, where autonomy, individuality, complexity, uncertainty, ambiguity become characteristics inherent in the object. Where, above all, the term "self" carries with it the root of subjectivity.

From then on, one can conceive, without there being an impassable epistemological gulf, that self-reference leads to awareness of self, that reflexivity leads to reflection, in short, that what appears are "systems with such a high capacity of self-organization that they produce a mysterious quality called consciousness or self-awareness."[13]

But the subject also emerges with existential characteristics that have been highlighted since Kierkegaard. It carries in itself an irreducible individuality, a sufficiency (as a recursive being that always loops around on itself) and an insufficiency (as an "open" being unresolvable in itself). It carries in itself breaches, cracks, waste, death, the beyond.

So, our point of view supposes the world and recognizes the subject. Better, it positions one and the other in a reciprocal and inseparable way: the world cannot appear as such, in other words, as the horizon of an eco-system of eco-systems, the horizon of *physis*, without a thinking subject, the ultimate development of self-organizing complexity. But such a subject cannot appear except through a physical process, through which the phenomenon of self-organization developed, in a thousand steps, always conditioned by an eco-system becoming richer and vaster. And so the subject and the object emerge like two ultimate, inseparable consequences of the relation between the self-organizing system and the eco-system.

Here, we can see that systemism and cybernetics are the first stage of a rocket that allows the launching of a second stage, the theory of self-organization, which in turn fires off a third, epistemological, stage, that of the relation between subject and object.

From then on, we arrive without a doubt at a crucial point in Western physics and metaphysics, a point that, since the seventeenth century, brings the two together, and at the same time, irreducibly opposes them.

In effect, Western science was founded on the positivist elimination of the subject on the basis of the idea that objects exist independently of the subject, and could, therefore, be observed and explained in and of themselves, without reference to the subject. The idea of a universe made up of objects, purged of all value judgments, of all subjective deformations, thanks to experimental method and verification procedures, has permitted the prodigious development of modern science. Certainly, as Jacques Monod defined it so well, we are faced with a postulate, in other words, a bet about the nature of reality and of knowledge.

In this frame, the subject is either the "noise"—in other words, disruption, deformation, the error that must be eliminated to achieve objective knowledge—or it is a mirror, a simple reflection of the objective universe.

The subject is dismissed as disturbance or noise precisely because it is indescribable according to the criteria of objectivism. "There is nothing in our present theories of mind that permits us to logically distinguish between an object such as a stone, and a subject as a unit of consciousness, which appears to us as a pseudo-object if we lodge it in the body of an animal or a human, and call it Ego."[14] The subject becomes a ghost of the objective universe; it's the "mysterious X that defies description in terms of predicates applicable to any object contained in the universe."[15]

But driven from science, the subject takes its revenge in morals, metaphysics, and ideology. Ideologically, it is the fabric of humanism, the human religion considering that the subject reigns, or should reign, over a world of objects (to be possessed, manipulated, transformed). Morally, it is the essential seat of all ethics. Metaphysically, it is the ultimate or primary reality that reflects the object as a pale ghost or at best, a pathetic mirror of the structures of our understanding.

From all sides, gloriously or shamefully, implicitly or overtly, the subject has been transcendentalized. Excluded from the objective world, "subjectivity or consciousness (has been identified) with the concept of a transcendental that arrives from the Beyond."[16] King of the universe, guest of the universe, the subject spreads out in the kingdom unoccupied by science. To the positivist elimination of the subject, the other side responds with the metaphysical elimination of the object. The objective world dissolves in the thinking subject. Descartes was the first to have conjured up in all its radicality this duality that was to mark the modern West, positing the either/or alternative of the objective universe of res extensa, open to science, and the irresistible subjective cogito, irreducible first principle of reality.

Since then, effectively, the duality of the object and the subject is posited in terms of disjunction, of repulsion, of reciprocal annulment. The meeting of subject and object always cancels one of the two terms. Either the subject becomes noise—nonsense—or it is the object, at the edge of the world, that becomes noise. What does the objective world matter for those who hear the categorical imperative of moral law (Kant), for those who live the existential trembling of angst and the quest (Kierkegaard).

But these disjunctive/repulsive terms mutually canceling each other out are at the same time inseparable. The part of reality that is hidden by the object reflects the subject, the part of reality hidden by the subject reflects the object. Furthermore, there is no object except in relation to a subject (who observes, isolates, defines, thinks), and there is no subject except in relation to an objective environment (which allows the subject to recognize itself, to define itself, to think itself, etc., but also to exist.)

The object and the subject, each left to their own devices, are insufficient concepts. The idea of a purely objective universe is deprived not only of a subject, but of an environment, of a beyond. It is extremely impoverished, closed in on itself, resting on nothing more than the postulate of objectivity, surrounded by an unfathomable void, and at its center, where the thought of this universe is, there is another unfathomable void. The concept of subject, stunted at an empirical level or hyper-atrophied at a transcendental level, is in turn deprived of environment and, annihilating the world, it closes itself up in solipsism.

And so appears the great paradox. Subject and object are indissociable, but our way of thinking excludes one through the other, leaving us only free to choose, according to the moments of the day, between the metaphysical subject and the positivist object. And when the scientist chases from his or her mind concerns about career, jealousies and professional rivalries, spouse and lover, to focus on guinea pigs, the subject suddenly cancels itself out, by a phenomenon so unbelievable that it might be found in a science fiction story about the passage between one universe and another via some hyperspace. It becomes "noise" while being the seat of objective knowledge, because the scientist is the observer. This observer, this scientist who is precisely working on the object, has disappeared. The great mystery, namely, that scientific objectivity must necessarily appear in the mind of a human subject, is completely avoided, pushed aside, or stupidly reduced to the theme of self-reflection.

But this theme of reflection is richer than it first appears as soon as we cease our ostrich solution when faced with a screaming contradiction. It is a theme that raises the paradox of a double mirror. In effect, the positivist concept of the object makes of consciousness both a reality (mirror) and an absence of reality (reflection). One could, in fact, propose that consciousness, no doubt in an uncertain way, reflects the world. But if the subject reflects the world, that could also mean that the world reflects the subject. Why is "our feeling, persevering, thinking Ego found nowhere in our world picture?" asked Schrödinger. And he answered that it is "because it is itself the world picture; it is identical with the whole and by this, cannot be contained as a part of that whole."[17] Therefore, the object can be a mirror for the subject as well as the subject for the object. Schrödinger also showed the double face of the subject's consciousness: "on one side, it is the theater and the only theater where the totality of world process takes place, on the other, it is an insignificant accessory that could be absent without having any effect whatsoever on the whole."[18]

Finally, it is interesting to notice that the subject/object disjunction, in turning the subject into "noise," into an "error," also creates a disjunction between determinism, characteristic of the world of objects, and the indetermination that has become characteristic of the subject.

If we valorize the object, we valorize determinism. But if we valorize the subject, then indeterminism becomes rich, swarming with possibilities, with freedom, and so it takes the shape of the key paradigm of the West. The object is knowable, determinable, isolatable, and by consequence, manipulable. It holds objective truth and, because of this, is all for science; but, manipulable by technics, it is nothing. The subject is the unknown because it is indeterminate, because it is a mirror, because it is foreign, because it is a totality. Therefore, in the science of the West, the subject is the all-nothing—nothing exists without it, but everything excludes it. It is the fabric of all truth, but at the same time it is nothing more than "noise" and error next to the object.

Our path was cleared on one side by micro-physics where subject and object become relational, but remain incongruent one to the other, and on the other by cybernetics and the concept of self-organization. We have already extracted ourselves from the determinism/randomness duality because the self-organizing system needs indetermination and randomness for its own self-determination. By the same token, we escape the disjunction and cancellation of the subject and the object because we are starting from the concept of open systems, which already, at its most elementary level, implies the consubstantial presence of the environment, in other words, the interdependence between the system and the eco-system.

If I start from a self-eco-organizing system, and I work my way up from complexity to complexity, I finally arrive at a reflecting subject that is none other than myself, trying to think the subject-object relation. And, inversely, if I start from this reflecting subject to find its foundation or at least its origin, I find my society and the history of this society in the evolution of self-eco-organizing humanity.

And so the world is interior to our mind, which is inside the world. Subject and object in this process are constitutive of each other. This doesn't lead to a unifying and harmonious vision; we can't escape from a generalized principle of uncertainty. In the same way that as in microphysics, the observer disturbs the object, which disturbs the perception, in the same way the notions of object and subject are profoundly disturbed each by the other: each opens a crack in the other. There is, we will see, a fundamental, ontological, uncertainty in the relation between the subject and the environment, that only the absolute (false) ontological decision can settle concerning the reality of the object or of the subject. A new conception emerges both from the complex relation between the subject and the object, and the insufficient and incomplete character of the two notions. The subject must remain open, deprived of all decidability in itself; the object itself must remain open toward the subject and toward its environment, which, in turn, necessarily opens and continues to open beyond the limits of our understanding.

This restriction of concepts, this ontological crack, this regression of objectivity, of determinism, seems to carry, as its first harvest, the general regression of knowledge, uncertainty.

However this necessary restriction is a stimulus to growth. The ontological error was to close, in other words to petrify, the basic concepts of science (and philosophy). We must, on the contrary, open up the possibility that is at the same time richer while less certain. One can extrapolate, from the whole of science, and more broadly from the problem of knowledge, what Niels Bohr said after the introduction of the quantum in microphysics: "At first glance, this situation could appear very regrettable; but often in the course of the history of science, when new ideas reveal the limits of ideas whose universal value has never been contested, we are rewarded: our vision broadens, and we become able to link phenomena that before could seem contradictory."[19]

COHERENCE AND EPISTEMOLOGICAL OPENING

The theoretical effort I am outlining here naturally opens up onto the subject-object relation. It opens up both to the relation between the researcher (in this case, myself) and the object of his knowledge. Consubstantially it carries a principle of uncertainty and self-reference, it carries in itself, a self-critical and self-reflective principle. Through these two traits, it already carries in itself its own epistemological potential.

Epistemology needs to find a point of view that can consider our own knowledge as an object of knowledge, in other words, a meta-point of view, as in the case when a meta-language constitutes itself to consider the language that has become object. This meta-point of view must at the same time allow for a critical self-consideration of knowledge, and enrich the reflexivity of the knowing subject.

Here, we can sketch out the epistemological point of view that allows us to check, in other words, to critique, to surpass, and to reflect on our theory. It is, first of all, the point of view that situates us eco-systemically by becoming aware of the determinations and conditioning of the environment. We must consider:

1. The point of view that, by situating us in the natural eco-system, incites us to examine the biological characteristics of knowledge. This biology of knowledge obviously concerns cerebral forms that are a priori constitutive of human knowledge, and also its learning modalities through dialogue with the environment.
2. The point of view that situates us in our social eco-system here and now, which produces ideological determinations/conditioning of our knowledge.

And so, the consideration of the social system allows us to distance ourselves from ourselves, to look at ourselves from the outside, to objectify ourselves, that is to say at the same time, to recognize our subjectivity.

But this necessary effort is insufficient. There is, between the human cerebral system and its environment, a fundamental uncertainty that cannot be overcome. In fact, the biology of knowledge shows us that there is no device in the human brain that allows us to distinguish perception from hallucination, the real from the imaginary. There is also an uncertainty about our knowledge of the external world, given that it is inscribed in patterns of organization, the most fundamental of which are innate. On the side of the sociology of knowledge, we also arrive at an irreducible uncertainty: the sociology of knowledge allows us to relativize our concepts, to situate ourselves in the play of social forces, but it will tell us nothing certain on the intrinsic validity of our theory.

We need, therefore, another meta-system, this time of a logical nature, that examines the theory from the perspective of internal consistency. Here, we enter into the classical field of epistemology, but we come up against the problem of Gödelian undecidability. Gödel's theorem, seemingly limited to mathematical logic, is applicable a fortiori to all theoretical systems. It shows that, in a formalized system, there is at least one proposition that is undecidable. This undecidability opens a crack in the system, leading to uncertainty. Certainly, the undecidable proposition can be proven in another system, even a meta-system, but these too will contain a logical crack.

There is in this a kind of unsurpassable barrier to the culmination of knowledge, but we can also see there an incitement to surpass knowledge by the construction of a meta-system, a movement, which, from meta-system to meta-system, causes knowledge to progress, but always, at the same time, causes new ignorance and new unknowns to appear.

Here we can see how this uncertainty is linked to the theory of open systems. In fact, the meta-system of an open system cannot be other than open itself, and in turn, also needs a meta-system. There is, therefore, a correspondence between the open perspective at the foundation of the theory of open systems and the infinite crack opened at the summit of every cognitive system by Gödel's theorem.

All this incites us toward an open epistemology. Epistemology, we must underline in this time of "police" epistemology, is not a strategic point that is occupied to control all knowledge with sovereign power, to reject all adversarial theories, and to give one a monopoly on verification, and, therefore, on the truth. Epistemology is not pontifical nor judiciary. It is the place of both uncertainty and dialogics. In fact, all the uncertainties we have raised must confront and correct each another; there must be dialogue, without, however, hoping to stop the ultimate crack with an ideological Band-Aid.

Here, Niels Bohr's expression cited earlier, according to which a limitation on knowledge is transformed into a broadening of knowledge, takes on its full epistemological and theoretical meaning.

All important progress of knowledge, as Kuhn has indicated, necessarily happens by the shattering and rupture of closed systems, which do not have the capacity to go beyond themselves. Therefore, as soon as a theory proves incapable of integrating observations that are increasingly important, a veritable revolution occurs, shattering the system that created both its coherence and its closure. One theory substitutes the previous theory, and perhaps, integrates the previous theory, by annexing it and relativizing it.

But this vision of evolution as surpassing a system and creating a meta-system, which is itself surpassable, applies not only to scientific ideas, but also to living self-eco-organizing systems. And we find once more a coincidence necessary for our epistemo-theoretical liaison. The theory of self-organization naturally carries with it the principle and the possibility of an epistemology that, far from solipsistically closing in on itself, confirms and deepens these two fundamental aspects, openness and (self-) reflexivity, and its two fundamental relations, eco-systemic and meta-systemic.

Therefore, far from attempting a rigid unification, we can assure a supple but essential connection between systemic opening and Gödelian crack, between empirical uncertainty and theoretical undecidability, and between physical and thermodynamic opening and epistemological and theoretical opening.

Finally, we can give an epistemological meaning to our open conception of the subject/object relationship. It indicates to us that the object must be conceived in its eco-system and more broadly, in an open world (that knowledge can not fill) and in a meta-system: a theory to be elaborated in which one could integrate both subject and object.

The isolated subject closes itself into the unsurpassable difficulties of solipsism. The notion of subject holds no meaning except in an eco-system (natural, social, familial, etc.) and must be integrated in a meta-system. Each of the two notions, therefore, object and subject, to the extent that they are presented as absolutes, show an enormous, ridiculous, insurmountable gap. But if they recognize this gap, then the gap becomes an opening of one toward the other, opening toward the world, opening toward a possible surmounting of the either/or alternative, toward a possible progress of knowledge.

Let us recapitulate: the complex conception that we are trying to elaborate calls for and provides a means of self-criticism. It calls for, in a natural development, a second epistemological viewpoint. It carries truths that are biodegradable—in other words, mortal—and, at the same time, alive.

SCIENZA NUOVA

And so, passing through cybernetics, systems theory, and information theory, we have sketched out the discourse that we propose to develop. These preliminary thoughts schematize, not entirely in a chronological way, for sure, but in a fairly logical way, my own itinerary. It had me going into biology, to better get out, getting into systems theory, cybernetics, also to better get out, interrogating advanced sciences that put into question the old paradigm of disjunction/reduction/simplification.

This has served as a means to clear the ground and to reconsider theories rich with ignored treasures, but they have been theories of which the lighted facets reflect technocratic platitude (cybernetics, systems theory). At the same time, I can see that the discourse I am setting out on is already sketched out in all its parts, that most of the sketches are old, some as much as a lustrum (micro-physics), others already more than twenty years. I don't claim to carry this discourse to culmination (particularly because I demonstrated that it can only be unfinished). Proceeding by cracking, integration and reflection, I wanted to try to give it a face. I wanted to situate myself in a place of movement (and not the throne where arrogant doctrinaires claim to sit), in a complex thought that connects theory to methodology, to epistemology, and even to ontology.

In fact, as we can already see, the theory does not shatter during the passage from the physical to the biological, from the biological to the anthropological, even as it made, at each of these levels, a meta-systemic leap, from entropy to negentropy, from negative anthropology to anthropology (hypercomplexity). It calls for a methodology that is at the same time open (that integrates the preceding) and specific (description of complex units).

It supposes and makes explicit an ontology that not only puts the accent on relation rather than on substance but also puts the accent on emergence and on interference, as constitutive phenomena of the object. There is not only a formal network of relations, there are *realities*, but these are not essences, not of a single substance. They are rather composites, produced by systemic interplay, but at the same time endowed with a certain autonomy.

Finally, and above all, what we were looking for and believe we have found, is the hinge for fundamental research, the theoretical, methodological, and epistemological whole that is at once coherent and open. We believe it to be much more coherent than all other theories that spread out in so vast a domain but are reduced to incessantly repeating their generalities. We believe it more vast and more open than all other coherent theories. We believe it more logical and more vast than all other open theories (which fall into eclecticism, lacking a backbone.) We will attempt here a nontotalitarian, multidimensional discourse, theoretical but not doctrinal (doctrine is closed theory, self-sufficient, and, therefore, insufficient), open to uncertainty and to being surpassed. It is not ideal/idealist, knowing that the thing will never be totally enclosed in the concept, the world will never be imprisoned in the discourse.

This is the idea of scienza nuova. This term, that we borrow from Vico, in a different context and a different text, attempts to indicate that our effort is situated in a modification, a transformation, an enrichment of the current concept of science that, as Bronowski said, is "neither absolute, nor eternal." It is about a multidimensional transformation of what we mean by science, concerning what seems to constitute certain of its intangible imperatives, starting with the inescapability of disciplinary fragmentation and theoretical splitting.

FOR A UNITY OF SCIENCE

We posit at the same time the possibility and the necessity of a unity of science. Such a unity is obviously impossible and incomprehensible in the current frame where myriad data accumulate in the increasingly narrow and closed cells of a disciplinary hive. It is impossible in the frame where the great disciplines seem to correspond to essences and heterogeneous subjects: physics, biology, anthropology. But it is conceivable in the field of a generalized physis.

Such a unification would make no sense if it were only reductionist, reducing phenomena of complex organization to the simplest level of organization. It would be insipid if it were carried out by cloaking itself in catch-all generalities, like the word "system." It makes no sense unless it is capable of apprehending unity and diversity at the same time, continuity and rupture. However, it seems to us that this would be possible for a theory of self-eco-organization, that is open toward a general theory of physis. Physics, biology, and anthropology cease to be closed entities but do not lose their identity. The unity of science respects physics, biology, and anthropology but shatters physicism, biologism, anthropologism (fig. 2.1).

We see the difference with the attempt of a unity of science launched by logical positivism. Logical positivism could not avoid playing the role of an epistemological policeman forbidding us to look precisely where we must look today—toward the uncertain, the ambiguous, the contradictory.

As always, a theory that claims to be fundamental escapes the field of disciplines, and crosses over them, as did, each with its own blindness and its own arrogance, Marxism, Freudianism, and Structuralism.

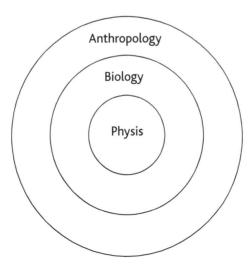

Figure 2.1

This is to say that the perspective here is transdisciplinary. Today, transdisciplinary means undisciplinary. An entire, enormous bureaucratized institution—science—a whole body of principles, resists the slightest questioning, rejects with violence and disdain as nonscientific all that does not correspond to the model.

But there is an uncertainty—a crack, an opening—in the concept of science. Any pretension to define the borders of science in an assured way, any pretension to a monopoly of science is by the same logic not scientific. I know that I will be reproached until death (my death and their death) for the innocent truths that I proffer here, but say it I must, because science has become blind in its capacity to monitor, foresee, even to conceive its social role, in its capacity to integrate, articulate, reflect on its own knowledge. If the human mind cannot effectively apprehend the enormous entirety of disciplinary knowledge, then something must change—either the human mind or disciplinary knowledge.

INTEGRATION OF THE REALITIES BANISHED
BY CLASSICAL SCIENCE

The new unity of science does not become meaningful except with the return of those evicted in the eighteenth and nineteenth centuries, who reintegrate the sciences, slowly or locally or on the sly. This banishment corresponded perhaps to a necessary parenthesis, which was, after all, heuristic because it allowed the extraordinary development of the sciences. However, perhaps it is also a very heavy handicap that, today, asphyxiates and smothers the new and necessary metamorphosis.

The issue, therefore, is not only recognizing the presence of chance, but of integrating chance, in its unpredictable character and in its character as historical events (Fr. *evenementialité*).[20] It is not about only localizing information in a statistical fashion but about considering its radical and polydimensional character, a concept that cannot be reduced to matter and energy. It is about always integrating the environment, even into the concept of the world. It is about integrating the self-eco-organized being, even into the concept of subject.

Minimally, it is about recognizing what has always passed in silence in the theories of evolution: innovation and creativity. Creativity has been recognized by Chomsky as a basic anthropological phenomenon. We must add that creativity marks all biological evolutions in a far more incredible way than historical evolution, which is still far from having rediscovered all the inventions of life, starting with the marvel of the cell.

Classical science rejected the accidental, the event, hazard, the individual. Each attempt to reintegrate them could not appear other than anti-scientific in the frame of the old paradigm. The old paradigm had rejected the cosmos and the subject. It had rejected the alpha and the omega to keep itself with the middle band. Since then, as we have gone forward in the macro (astronomy, theory of relativity) and the micro (particle physics), this middle band, this flying carpet, revealed itself to be moth-eaten and mythical. The essential problems, the great problems of knowledge, were always cast out and up to the heavens, becoming errant ghosts of philosophy. Mind, Freedom, Science, became more and more anemic, but the bankruptcy of this system of understanding was masked by its corresponding success as a system of manipulation.

The scienza nuova proposes something with incalculable consequences. It is simply this: the object must not only be appropriate to science, but science must be appropriate to its object.

BEYOND CLASSICAL EITHER/ OR ALTERNATIVES

In this line of thought, we see that classical alternatives lose their absolute character, or rather, change character. For "either/or" we substitute both "neither/ nor" and "both/and." And, as we have seen, this also applies to the opposition between unity/diversity, chance/necessity, quantity/quality, subject/ object. It also applies to holism/reductionism. In fact, reductionism has always provoked an opposing holistic current founded on the preeminence of the concept of globality or totality. But the totality is never anything more than a plastic bag enveloping whatever it found any way it could, and enveloping too well: the more the totality becomes full, the emptier it becomes. On the contrary, what we want to draw out, beyond reductionism and holism, is the idea of the complex unity, that links analytical-reductionist thinking and global thinking, in a dialogic whose premises we will propose later. This means that if reduction— the search for elementary, simple units, the decomposition of a system into its elements, the origination of the complex to the simple—will remain an essential characteristic of the scientific mind, it is no longer the only, nor, particularly, the last, word.

So, the scienza nuova does not destroy the classical alternatives, it doesn't bring a monist solution that would be like the essence of truth. But the alternative terms become antagonistic, contradictory, and at the same time complementary at the heart of a more ample vision, a vision that, in turn, will have to meet and confront new alternatives.

THE PARADIGMATIC TURNING POINT

We sense that we are approaching a considerable revolution (so considerable that perhaps it won't take place), in the great paradigm of Western science (and correlatively, in the metaphysics, which is sometimes its negative, sometimes its complement). Let us repeat that the flaws and the cracks are multiplying in this paradigm—but it is still holding together.

What affects a paradigm, that is, the vault key of a whole system of thought, affects the ontology, the methodology, the epistemology, the logic, and by consequence, the practices, the society, and the politics. The ontology of the West was founded on closed entities, such as substance, identity, (linear) causality, subject, object. These entities don't communicate amongst themselves. Oppositions provoke repulsion or canceling of a concept by another (like subject/object). "Reality" could be grasped by clear and distinct ideas.

In this sense, scientific methodology was reductionist and quantitative. It was Reductionist because it was necessary to arrive at nondecomposable elementary units, that alone could be grasped clearly and distinctly. It was quantitative because these discrete units could be the base of all computations. The logic of the West was a homeostatic logic, destined to maintain the equilibrium of the discourse by banning contradiction or deviation. It controlled or guided all developments in thinking but positioned itself as obviously beyond development. Epistemology, therefore, always played the role of the verifying border patrol or the forbidding policeman.

Imagination, illumination, and creation, without which the progress of science would not have been possible, only entered science on the sly. They could not be logically identified, and were always epistemologically condemnable. They are spoken of in the biographies of great scientists, but never in manuals and treatises, whose somber compilation, like subterranean layers of coal, was constituted by the fossilization and compression of what were initially fantasies, hypotheses, proliferations of ideas, inventions, and discoveries.

The Western paradigm, no doubt a fecund child of the schizophrenic Cartesian dichotomy and the clergyman's Puritanism, also commands the double aspect of Western praxis, on the one hand, it is anthropocentric, ethnocentric, egocentric as soon as it concerns the subject (because it is founded on the self-adoration of the subject: human, national, ethnic, individual); on the other hand and correlatively, manipulative, icy, with an "objective" veneer as soon as it addresses the object. This is not unrelated to the identification of rationalization with efficiency, an efficiency with results that are easily inscribed in accounting books. It is inseparable from a whole classifying, reifying tendency, a tendency countered sometimes strongly, sometimes barely, by apparently "irrational", "sentimental", romantic, poetic, counter tendencies.

In fact, the part of human reality (and perhaps of the reality of the world) that is at the same time pregnant and heavy, ethereal and dreamlike was taken on by the irrational—part cursed, part blessed—where poetry filled and over-flowed with its essences, which, if it were filtered and distilled someday, could and should be called science.

We glimpse here the radical nature and scope of the paradigmatic reform. In a way, it is about what is the simplest, most elementary, most childlike: to change reasoning's point of departure, the relations of association and repulsion among a few initial concepts, on which, the whole structure of reasoning and all possible discursive developments, depend. And this, of course, is what is most difficult. Nothing is easier than to explain something difficult from sim-ple premises admitted by the speaker and the listener, nothing is simpler that to follow subtle reasoning on paths that carry the same markers and signaling systems. However, nothing is more difficult than to modify the foundational concept, the massive and elementary idea that supports the whole of the intel-lectual edifice.

For it is obviously the whole structure of the system of thought that is find-ing itself thoroughly shaken and transformed. It is the whole of an enormous superstructure of ideas that is collapsing. This is what we must prepare for.

3

THE PARADIGM
OF COMPLEXITY

We must not believe that the question of complexity is only being asked today because of some new scientific developments. We must see complexity where it generally might seem absent—in daily life, for example.

This particular complexity has been perceived and described in the novels of the nineteenth century and those of beginning of the twentieth century. During this same era, science was trying to eliminate the individual and the singular, retaining only general laws and simple and closed identities. Science even rejected time from its vision of the world. The novel, on the contrary (Balzac in France, Dickens in England) shows us singular beings in their context and in their time. The novel shows us that the most ordinary of lives is, in fact, a life in which everyone plays several social roles, depending on whether she or he is at home, at work, with friends, or with strangers. We see that each being has a multiplicity of identities, a multiplicity of personalities in the self, a world of fantasies and dreams accompanying life. For example, the theme of the internal monologue, so powerful in Faulkner's writing, is itself a part of this complexity. This inner speech, this constant talk, is revealed by literature, by the novel, which at the same time also reveals to us how little one knows oneself: We call this *self-deception*, lying to ourselves. We know ourselves only as an appearance of self. We are mistaken about our selves. Even the most sincere writers, such as Jean-Jacques Rousseau and Chateaubriand, always forgot, in their effort to be sincere, something important about themselves.

The ambivalent relation with those different from ourselves, the veritable mutations of personality we find in Dostoyevski, the fact that one is carried away in the story without really knowing how, like Fabrice Del Dongo or Prince André, the fact that the same being transformed in time as in *Remembrance of Things Past* and particularly at the end of *Time Regained* by Proust, all this indicates that it is not simply society that is complex, but each atom in the human world.

At the same time, in the nineteenth century, science has an exactly opposite ideal. This ideal affirms itself in Laplace's vision of the world at the beginning of the nineteenth century. Scientists, from Descartes to Newton, tried to conceive of a universe that was a perfect deterministic machine. But Newton, like Descartes, needed God to explain how this perfect world was made. Laplace eliminated God. When Napoleon asked him, "But M. de Laplace, what do you do with God in your system?" Laplace answered "Sire, I have no need for that hypothesis." For Laplace, the world is a truly perfect deterministic machine, sufficient unto itself. He supposed that a demon possessing intelligence and almost infinite senses could know all events, past and future. In effect, this conception that thought it could do without God had introduced in its world the very attributes of divinity: perfection, absolute order, immortality, and eternity. It is this world that is going to derail, then disintegrate.

THE PARADIGM OF SIMPLICITY

To understand the problem of complexity, we must first know that there is a paradigm of simplicity. The word *paradigm* is used frequently. In our conception, a paradigm is made up of a certain kind of extremely strong logical relation between master notions, key notions, key principles. This relation and these principles command all propositions that unconsciously obey its empire.

The paradigm of simplicity puts order in the universe and chases out disorder. Order is reduced to one law, one principle. Simplicity can see either the one or the many, but it can't see that the One is perhaps at the same time Many. The principle of simplicity either separates that which is linked (disjunction), or unifies that which is diverse (reduction).

Let's take human beings as an example. Humans are obviously biological beings. At the same time, they are obviously cultural and meta-biological. They live in a universe of language, ideas, and awareness. But in the paradigm of simplification, these two realities, the biological reality and the cultural reality, are either disjoined or the more complex is reduced to the least complex. We will, therefore, study human biology in the biology department, in terms of anatomy, physiology, and so on, and human culture in the departments of the human and social sciences. We will study the brain as a biological organ, and we will study the mind as a psychological function or reality. We forget that one doesn't exist without the other. More, that one is, at the same time, the other, even though they are being addressed by different terms and different concepts.

With this will to simplification, scientific knowledge gave itself the mission of revealing the simplicity hidden behind the apparent multiplicity and apparent disorder of phenomena. Maybe because they were deprived of a God in whom they could no longer believe, scientists unconsciously needed to be reassured. Although they knew themselves to live in a material, mortal world without salvation, they needed to know that there was something that is perfect and eternal: the universe itself. This extremely powerful mythology, obsessive as well as hidden, animated the movement of physics. We have to acknowledge that this mythology was fertile because the search for the great law of the universe led to the discovery of major laws such as gravity, electromagnetism, and strong and then weak nuclear interactions. To this day, scientists and physicists are trying to find the nexus between these different laws that would make a truly single law.

The same obsession led to the search for the elementary building block of the universe. We first thought we had found it in the molecule. The development of instruments of observation revealed that the molecule itself was made of atoms. Then we realized that the atom was itself a very complex system, composed of a nucleus and electrons. Then the particle became the primary unit. Then we realized that particles were themselves phenomena that could be theoretically divided into quarks. And, just when we thought we had found the elementary unit with which our universe was built, it disappeared as a unit. It is now a complex, fuzzy entity that cannot be isolated. The obsession with simplicity has led to the scientific adventure of discoveries impossible to conceive of in terms of simplicity.

In addition, in the nineteenth century, there was that major event: the eruption of disorder in the physical universe. In effect, the second principle of thermodynamics, formulated by Carnot and Clausius, began as a principle of degradation of energy. The first principle that is the principle of the conservation of energy, is accompanied by the principle that energy degrades in the form of heat. All activity, all work produces heat. In other words, all use of energy tends to degrade that energy.

Then we realized, with Boltzmann, that what we were calling heat was in reality the disorderly movement of molecules or of atoms. Anyone can verify, starting with the heating of a container of water, that a tremor appears, a whirling of molecules. Some evaporate into the atmosphere until they all disperse. In fact, what happens is total disorder. Thus, there is disorder in the physical universe, linked to all work, to all transformation.

ORDER AND DISORDER IN THE UNIVERSE

At the beginning of the twentieth century, the reflection on the universe came up against a paradox. On one side, the second principle of thermodynamics indicated that the universe tends toward general entropy—in other words, to maximal disorder—and on the other side, it seemed that in the same universe things organize themselves, complexify, and develop.

As long as we limited ourselves to the planet, we might have thought that it was about the difference between living organization and physical organization. Physical organization tends toward degradation, but living organization, based on a specific, much more noble, substance, tends towards development. We forgot two things: First, how is this physical organization constituted? How are the stars constituted, how are molecules constituted? Second we forgot that life is progress at the expense of the death of individuals. Biological evolution is at the expense of the death of innumerable species. There are many more species that have disappeared since the origin of life than have survived. Degradation and disorder apply to life as well.

So, the dichotomy was no longer possible. It took these last decades for us to realize that disorder and order, although enemies, cooperate in a certain way to organize the universe.

We realize this, for example, in Bénard's whirlpools. Let us take a cylindrical container with a liquid heated from below. At a certain temperature, the turbulence, rather than increasing, produces an organized whirlpool form of a stable character, forming regularly arranged hexagonal cells on the surface.

Often, in the meeting between a flow and an obstacle, a whirlpool is created, that is, a constant, organized form that unceasingly reconstructs itself. The union of flow and counter-flow produces this organized form that will last indefinitely, at least as long as the flow lasts and as long as the obstacle is there. That is to say, an organizational order (whirlpool) can emerge from a process that produces disorder (turbulence).

This idea was amplified cosmically when, in 1960–1966, we reached the increasingly plausible opinion that our universe, which we knew was in the process of dilation with Hubble's discovery of the expansion of galaxies, was also a universe where isotropic rays radiated from all sides, as if this radiation were the fossil residue of some sort of initial explosion. From this arose the dominant theory in the current world of astrophysicists, of the origin of the universe in a giant deflagration—a big bang. That leads us to a remarkable idea: the universe began as a disintegration, and in disintegrating, it organized itself. In effect, it is during this intense caloric agitation—heat is agitation, whirling, movement in all directions—that particles are formed, and that certain particles will unite with others.

In this way, the nuclei of helium, hydrogen and are created. And then other processes, notably gravity, assemble the dust of particles, and this dust will concentrate more and more until it reaches a moment when, with the increasing heat, an explosive temperature is produced and stars are ignited, and the stars themselves self-organize between implosion and explosion.

Moreover, we can suppose that inside these stars, in extremely disorganized conditions, three nuclei of helium will sometimes unite to form a carbon atom. In the succession of suns, there will have been enough carbon so that, finally, on a little eccentric planet, Earth, there was this necessary material without which there would not be what we call life.

We see how agitation and random encounters are necessary to the organization of the universe. One can say of the world that it organizes itself through its disintegration. Here is a typically complex idea in the sense that we have to bring together two notions—order and disorder—that logically seem to exclude each other. In addition, we might think that the complexity of this idea is even more fundamental. In fact, the universe was born of an unspeakable moment, which bore time out of non-time, space out of non-space, matter out of non-matter. We arrive by entirely rational means at ideas that carry a fundamental contradiction.

The complexity of the order/disorder/organization relationship appears, therefore, when we empirically notice that disorderly phenomena are necessary in certain conditions. In certain cases they are necessary for the production of organized phenomena, particularly those contributing to the growth of organization.

Biological order is a more developed order than physical order. It is an order that develops with life. At the same time, the world of life contains and tolerates a lot more disorder than the world of physics. In other words, disorder and order act incrementally on each other at the heart of an organization that has complexified.

We could take Heraclitus's famous words, which, seven centuries before Christ, pronounced in a lapidary way: "living from death, dying from life." Today, we know that this is not a futile paradox. Our organisms live only from the incessant work during which the molecules of our cells degrade. Not only do the molecules of our cells degrade, but the cells themselves die. Endlessly, throughout our lives, many times over, our cells are renewed, with the apparent exception of our brain cells and probably certain hepatic cells.

In a way, to live is to endlessly die and to rejuvenate. In other words, we live from the death of our cells, as society lives from the death of individuals, which allows it to rejuvenate. But by dint of rejuvenation, we get old, and the process of rejuvenation falls apart, derails, and in actuality, we live from death and we die from life.

Today, physics' conception of the universe makes it impossible to conceive of it in simple terms. Micro-physics has encountered the primary paradox in which the very notion of matter has lost its substance, where the notion of the particle finds itself in internal contradiction. Then it encounters a second paradox. This one is from the success of Aspect's experiment that demonstrated that particles can communicate at infinite speeds. In other words, in our universe, dominated by time and space, there is something that seems to escape time and space.

There is such complexity in the universe, such a series of contradictions have arisen, that certain scientists believe they have overcome this contradiction in what one could call a new metaphysics. These new metaphysicians seek in the mystics from the Far East, and particularly in the Buddhists, the experience of emptiness that is all, and the all that is nothing. They perceive there a sort of fundamental unity where everything is related, everything is in harmony in a way, and they hold a reconciled vision, I would say a euphoric vision, of the world.

In doing this, in my perspective, they escape from complexity because complexity is in a place where one cannot overcome a contradiction or even a tragedy. In certain aspects, contemporary physics has discovered that some things escape time and space, but that does not negate the fact that, at the same time, we are unquestionably in time and in space.

We cannot reconcile these two ideas. Should we accept them as they are? Accepting complexity means accepting a contradiction, and the idea that we cannot mask contradictions with a euphoric vision of the world.

Of course, our world contains harmony, but this harmony is linked to disharmony. This is exactly what Heraclitus said: there is harmony in disharmony, and vice versa.

SELF-ORGANIZATION

It is difficult to conceive of the complexity of reality. Some physicists have fortunately abandoned the old naïve materialism in which substance was endowed with all productive virtues, because this substantial matter has disappeared. Unfortunately they replaced matter with mind, and this generalized spiritualism is not much better than generalized materialism. They come together in a unifying and simplifying vision of the universe. I spoke of physics, but we could also speak of biology. Today biology has come, in my view, to the doors of complexity by not dissolving the individual in the general.

We thought that there was no science other than a science of the general. Today, physics situates us in a singular cosmos, and the biological sciences tell us that species are not a general framework in which individuals are born, but that a species is itself a very precise, singular pattern, a producer of singularities. In addition, the individuals in the same species are very different from each other. But we must understand that there is something more than singularity, or difference from one individual to the next. This something is the fact that each individual is a subject.

The word Subject is one of the most difficult, one of the most misunderstood words in existence because in the traditional view of science, where everything is deterministic, there is no subject, there is no consciousness, there is no autonomy.

If we leave behind a strict determinism, and conceive of a universe in which what is created is not only created out of chance and disorder but in self-organizing processes—that is to say where each system creates its own determinations and its own finalities—we can begin, minimally, to understand autonomy. Then we can begin to understand what "subject" means.

To be a subject, doesn't necessarily mean to be conscious. Neither does it mean to have affect or feelings, even though obviously human subjectivity develops with affect, with feelings. To be "subject" is to put oneself in the center of one's own world. It is to occupy the space of "I" for oneself. It is obvious that each one of us can say "I." Everyone can say "I", but one can only say "I" for oneself. No one can say it for another, even for a homozygotic twin, who resembles one exactly; one will say "I" for oneself, and not for one's twin.

The possibility of saying "I," of being subject, is to occupy a site, a position in which one places oneself in the center of one's own world, to be able to act upon it and upon oneself. This is what we call egocentrism. Of course, individual complexity is such that when we put ourselves at the center of our world, we also bring in our relations, that is to say, our parents, our children, our fellow citizens, and we are capable even of sacrificing our lives for them. Our egocentrism can be incorporated in a larger, communitarian subjectivity. The concept of subject must be complex.

To be subject is to be autonomous while remaining dependent. It is to be provisional, intermittent, uncertain. It is to be almost everything for oneself and almost nothing for the universe.

AUTONOMY

The notion of human autonomy is complex because it depends on cultural and social conditions. To be ourselves, we need to learn a language, a culture, knowledge, and this culture itself needs to be varied enough to allow us a choice among the stock of existing ideas, and to think in an autonomous way. So this autonomy is nourished by dependence. We depend on an education, a language, a culture, a society, a brain, which is itself the product of genetic programming, and we depend also on our genes.

We depend on our genes, and in a certain way, we are also possessed by our genes, because they never cease to dictate to our organism the means to continue to live. Reciprocally, we possess genes that possess us, that is to say we are capable, because of our genes, to have a brain, to have a mind, to be able to take from a culture the elements that interest us, and to develop our own ideas. There, too, we must return to literature, to those novels (like, quite appropriately, *The Possessed*) that show us to what extent we are both autonomous and possessed.

The Origin of Consciousness in the Breakdown of the Bicameral Mind [21] is certainly a debatable book, but it is interesting because of the following idea: in ancient civilizations, individuals had two noncommunicating chambers in their brain. One chamber was occupied by power: the king, theocracy, the gods. The other chamber was occupied by the daily life of the individual, by particular personal worries. Then, at a certain moment, in the ancient Greek polis, there was a break in the wall that separated the two chambers. Consciousness originated in this communication.

To this day, we have these two chambers inside us. We continue, in a part of us, to be possessed. Most of the time, we are not aware that we are possessed. This is the case, for example, of the striking experience in which a subject is submitted to a double hypnotic suggestion. We tell the subject who is a smoker and has not asked to stop smoking: "Starting tomorrow you will stop smoking." We add, "Tomorrow you will take such and such a route to go to work," a totally unusual route for this person. Then we erase these injunctions from memory. The next morning, the subject wakes up and says: "I'm going to stop smoking. In fact, it'll be a good thing, because it'll be easier to breathe, I'll avoid cancer. . . ." Then he says to himself, "To reward myself, I'm going to take such and such a street, there's a pastry shop there, and I'll buy myself a cake." This is of course the route that had been suggested.

What is interesting to us here is that he had the impression of having freely decided to stop smoking, to have rationally decided to take that particular route when there was no real reason to go there. How often we have the impression of being free when we are not free. At the same time, we are capable of freedom, as we are capable of examining hypotheses about behavior, to make choices, to make decisions. We are a mixture of autonomy, of freedom, of heteronomy and I would even say of possession by hidden forces beyond those simply brought to light by the psychoanalyst. This is one of the peculiarly human complexities.

COMPLEXITY AND COMPLETENESS

Complexity appears initially like some sort of hole, as a form of confusion or difficulty. There are, of course, several kinds of complexities. I say complexity out of convenience. But there are complexities related to disorder, and other complexities related to logical contradictions.

We can say of complexity that it arises in part from the empirical world, from uncertainty, from the inability to be certain about everything, to form a law, to conceive of an absolute order. It arises from something logical, that is to say from our inability to avoid contradictions.

In the classical view, when a contradiction appears in reasoning, it is a sign of error. You have to back up and take a different line of reasoning. However, in a complex view, when one arrives via empirical rational means at contradictions, this points not to an error but rather to the fact that we have reached a deep layer of reality that, precisely because of its depth, cannot be translated into our logic.

In this way, complexity is different from completion. It is often believed that the defenders of complexity claim to have complete visions of things. Why would they think that? Because it is true that we think that one can't isolate objects from each other. In a way, everything is interdependent. If you have the sense of complexity, you have the sense of solidarity. In addition, you have the sense of the multidimensional character of all reality.

The non-complex vision of the human and social sciences, holds that there is a separate economic reality, a psychological reality, a demographic reality, and so on. The categories created by the universities are considered real, but one forgets, for example, that in economics there are human needs and desires. Behind the money, there is a whole world of passion, there is human psychology. Even in what are considered strictly economic phenomena we find crowd phenomena, phenomena like panic, as we have regularly seen on Wall Street and elsewhere. The economic dimension contains the other dimensions and there is no reality that we can comprehend with a single dimension.

Consciousness of multidimensionality leads us to the idea that any unidimensional vision, all specialist and fragmented vision, is impoverished. It must be reconnected to other dimensions. This is the source of the belief that complexity can be identified as completeness.

In one way, I would say that the aspiration to complexity carries in it an aspiration to completeness, because we say that everything is interdependent and everything is multidimensional. But, in another way, consciousness of complexity makes us understand that we can never escape uncertainty and we can never have total knowledge because "totality is nontruth."

We are condemned to uncertain thought, a thought riddled with holes, a thought that has no foundation of absolute certainty. But, despite these dramatic conditions, we are capable of thinking. At the same time, we should not confuse complexity and complication. Complication, which is the extreme confusion of interretroactions, is one aspect, one of the elements of complexity. If, for example, a bacterium is already much more complicated than all the factories on the outskirts of Montreal, it is obvious that complication itself is linked to complexity that allows it to tolerate disorder within itself, to fight off its aggressors, to have the quality of a subject, and so forth. Complexity and complication are not two antinomial facts and they cannot be reduced to one another. Complication is one of the constituents of complexity.

REASON, RATIONALITY AND RATIONALIZATION

Now I come to the instruments that will allow us to know the complex universe. These instruments are obviously of a rational nature. But here we must also carry out a complex self-criticism of the notion of "reason."

Reason corresponds to a will to have a coherent vision of phenomena, of things, of the universe. Reason has an incontestably logical aspect. But, here as well, we can distinguish between rationality and rationalization.

Rationality is play, it is the incessant dialogue between our mind that creates logical structures, applies them to the world, in dialogue with the real world. When the world is not in agreement with our logical system, we must admit that our logical system is insufficient, that it encounters only a part of reality. Rationality, in a way, never has the ambition to exhaustively hold the totality of reality in a logical system, but it has the will to dialogue with what resists it. As Shakespeare said, there are more things in the world than there are in our philosophy. The universe is much richer than our brain structures can conceive, however developed it may be.

What is rationalization? A word very accurately used in pathology by Freud and many other psychiatrists. Rationalization consists of wanting to enclose reality in a coherent system. And everything that, in reality, contradicts this coherent system is put aside, forgotten, seen as an illusion or appearance.

Here we realize that rationality and rationalization have exactly the same source, but in developing, they become enemies of one another. It is very difficult to know at what moment we slip from rationality into rationalization; there is no border; there is no alarm. We have an unconscious tendency to push out of our minds what contradicts it, in politics as in philosophy. We will minimize or reject contrary arguments. We will focus selective attention on what favors our idea and selective inattention to what is unfavorable. Rationalization often develops even in the minds of scientists.

Paranoia is a classic form of delusional rationalization. You see someone who looks strangely at you, for example, and if you have a bit of a maniacal mind, you will suppose that it is a spy following you. So, you look at these people suspecting them of being spies, and those people, seeing your strange way of looking at them, look at you even more strangely, and you find yourself increasingly rationally surrounded by more and more spies.

There are no clear cut borders between paranoia, rationalization, and rationality. We must pay attention incessantly. The philosophers of the eighteenth century, in the name of reason, had a rather nonrational view of what myths were, of what religion was. They believed that religions and the gods had been made up by the priests to fool people. They didn't realize the depth and the reality of religious and mythological power in human beings. In doing so, they slipped into rationalization, that is to say, into a simplistic explanation of what their reason was unable to comprehend. It took new developments of reason to begin to understand myth. For this to happen, it was necessary for reason to become self-critical. We must incessantly fight against the deification of reason even as it is our only trustworthy instrument of knowledge, under the condition of being not only critical but also self-critical.

I underline the importance of this. At the beginning of the century, Western anthropologists, like Lévy-Bruhl in France, studied societies that they believed to be "primitive", and today we more accurately call "hunter-gatherer societies." These societies were our human prehistory, societies of a few hundred individuals who, during tens of thousands of years, have, in a way, constituted humanity. Lévy-Bruhl saw these so-called primitives, with the idea of his own Western-centric reason of the period, as childish and irrational beings.

He didn't ask himself the question that Wittgenstein pondered when he asked, reading the Frazer's *Golden Bough*: "How is it that all these savages, who spend their time practicing sorcery, propitiatory rites, witchcraft, representation, and so on, don't forget to create real arrows with real bows, with real strategies."[22] In fact, these societies we call primitive have a great rationality, embodied, in fact, in all their practices, in their knowledge of the world, embodied and mixed in with other things, in magic, in religion, in the belief in spirits, and so forth. We ourselves live in a culture that has developed certain sectors of rationality, like philosophy or science. We also live imbued with myths and magic of another kind. Therefore, we need a self-critical rationality, a rationality that exercises an incessant exchange with the empirical world, the only correction to logical madness.

Humanity has two types of madness. One is obviously very visible, it's the madness of absolute incoherence, of onomatopoeia, of words spoken randomly. The other is much less visible: it is the madness of absolute coherence. Against this second madness, the resource is self-critical rationality and recourse to experience.

Philosophy could never have been able to conceive of the formidable complexity of the actual universe, of the kind we have observed with quanta, quasars, black holes, with its incredible origins and its uncertain future. No thinker could have imagined that a bacterium could be of such extreme complexity. We need a constant dialogue with discovery. The virtue of science that keeps it from succumbing to madness is that new data arrives continuously and leads it to modifying its visions and its ideas.

THE NECESSITY OF MACRO-CONCEPTS

I'd like to conclude on a couple of principles that can help us to think about the complexity of reality. First of all, I think that we need macro-concepts. Just as an atom is a constellation of particles, just as the solar system is a constellation around a star, so we also need to think through constellations and solidarity of concepts. In addition, we need to know that in important things, concepts are not defined by their boundaries but by their cores. This is an anti-cartesian idea, in the sense that Descartes thought that distinction and clarity were the intrinsic characteristics of the truth of an idea.

Let's take love and friendship. We can clearly recognize their core of love and friendship, but there is also friendship in love and love in friendship. There are, therefore, intermediates, mixtures of love and friendship; there is not a clear boundary. One should never seek to define important things by their boundaries, because boundaries are always blurred, are always interfering. One must seek to define the heart, and this definition often requires macro-concepts.

THREE PRINCIPLES

I would say, finally, that there are three principles that can help us to think of complexity. The first is the principle that I call dialogic. Let's take the example of living organization. It is born, without a doubt, in the encounter between two types of chemico-physical entities: a stable kind that can reproduce and whose stability can carry a memory that becomes hereditary, such as DNA, and amino acids, which make proteins in multiple forms extremely unstable, which degrade but recreate themselves incessantly from messages that emanate from DNA.

In other words, there are two logics: one is the logic of an unstable protein, that lives in contact with the environment, which permits phenomenal existence, and the other that assures reproduction. These two principles are not simply juxtaposed, they are necessary to each other. The sexual process creates individuals who produce the sexual process. The two principles, that of transindividual reproduction and that of individual existence here and now, are complementary but also antagonistic. Sometimes, we are surprised to see mammals eat their young and sacrifice their offspring for their own survival. We ourselves can violently oppose ourselves to our family, preferring our own interests over those of our children or our parents. There is a dialogic between the two principles.

What I have said of order and disorder can be conceived in dialogic terms. Order and disorder are two enemies: one abolishes the other, but at the same time, in certain cases, they collaborate and produce organization and complexity. The dialogic principle allows us to maintain duality at the heart of unity. It associates two terms that are at the same time complementary and antagonistic.

The second principle is that of organizational recursion. For the meaning of this term, we might consider the process of a whirlpool. At every instant, a whirlpool is both product and producer. A recursive process is a process where the products and the effects are at the same time causes and producers of what produces them. We return to the example of the individual, the species and reproduction. We, as individuals, are products of a process of reproduction that precedes us. But once we have been produced, we become the producers of a process that will continue. This idea is also sociologically valid. Society is produced by interactions between individuals, but society, once it has been produced, feeds back on individuals, and produces them. If there were no society and its culture, no language, no acquired knowledge, we would not be human individuals. In other words, individuals produce society that produces individuals. We are at the same time products and producers. The recursive idea is, therefore, an idea that has broken away from the linear idea of cause and effect, of product/producer, or structure/superstructure, because everything that is

product comes back on what produces it in a cycle that is itself self-constitu-
tive, self-organizing, and self-producing.

The third principle is the holographic principle. In a physical hologram,
the smallest point of the hologram image contains the quasi-totality of information of the represented object. Not only is the part in the whole, but the whole
is in the part. The principle of the hologram is present in the biological world
and in the sociological world. In the biological world, each cell of our organism contains the totality of the genetic information of that organism. The idea
of the hologram surpasses both reductionism, which can only see the parts, and
holism, which only sees the whole. It is a bit like the idea formulated by Pascal:
"I cannot conceive the whole without conceiving the parts and I cannot conceive the parts without conceiving the whole." This apparently paradoxical idea
immobilizes the linear mind. But, in recursive logic, we know very well that
what we acquire in terms of knowledge about the parts feeds back on the
whole. What we learn about the emerging properties of the whole, a whole that
cannot exist without organization, feeds back on the parts. So we can enrich
knowledge of the parts through knowledge of the whole and knowledge of the
whole through knowledge of the parts, in a single productive movement of
knowledge.

So, the idea of the hologram is linked to the recursive idea, which is in part
linked to the dialogic idea. The anthropo-social relation is complex, because the
whole is in the part that is in the whole. From childhood, society as the whole
enters into us first through the first forbidden behaviors and the first family
injunctions: about cleanliness, dirt, being polite, and then through the injunctions of language and culture. The principle that no one can be ignorant of the
law imposes the strong presence of all things social on the individual, even if
the division of labor and compartmentalization of our lives means that no one
possesses the totality of social knowledge.

This is the source of the problem the sociologist has when reflecting on his
own status. He must abandon the divine point of view, the point of view from
some sort of raised throne from which to contemplate society. The sociologist
is a part of this society. The fact that he is the possessor of a sociological culture
does not put him at the center of society. On the contrary, he is a member of a
peripheral culture in the university and in the sciences. The sociologist is
dependent on a particular culture. Not only is she a part of the society, but on
top of it, without knowing it, she is possessed by all of society that tends to
deform her vision.

How do we get around this? Obviously, the sociologist can try to confront
her point of view with the view of other members of society, to learn about different types of societies, to possibly imagine viable societies that don't yet exist.
The only possible perspective from the point of view of complexity, and one
that appears very important, is to have meta-points of view of our society, exactly like the towers in a concentration camps, which were built to allow the cap-

tors to better look at the society and its outside environment. We can never reach the meta-system, by which I mean the superior system that would be meta-human and meta-social. Even if we could reach it, it wouldn't be an absolute system, because Tarski's logic as well as Gödel's theorem tell us that no system is capable of entirely explaining itself, nor of totally proving itself by itself.

In other words, every system of thought is open and contains a breach, a gap in the opening itself. But we have the possibility to hold meta-points of view. The meta-point of view is only possible if the observer-conceiver integrates himself or herself into the observation and the conception. This is why complex thought requires the integration of the observer and the conceiver in its observation and conception.

TOWARD COMPLEXITY

We can diagnose, in Western history, the domination of a paradigm that Descartes formulated. Descartes disjoined on the one side the domain of the subject, reserved for philosophy and interior meditation, and on the other side, the domain of the object out there, the domain of scientific knowledge, measure, and precision. Descartes formulated this principle of disjunction very well, and this disjunction has reigned in our universe. It has increasingly separated the culture we call humanist, the culture of literature, of poetry, of the arts, from scientific culture. The former culture, founded on reflection, can no longer nourish itself from sources of objective knowledge. The latter culture, founded on the specialization of knowledge, can't reflect on itself or think of itself.

The paradigm of simplification (disjunction and reduction) dominates our culture today and the reaction begins against its stronghold. But we can't pull it out and I can't pull it out; I can't pretend to pull a paradigm of complexity out of my pocket. A paradigm, although it must be formulated by someone—by Descartes, for example—is, fundamentally, the product of an entire cultural, historical, civilizational development. The paradigm of complexity will come from the collection of new conceptions, new visions, new discoveries, and new reflections that will align and come together. We are in an uncertain battle, and we don't know who will win. However, we can say that if simplifying thought is founded on the domination of two types of logical operations—disjunction and reduction—which are both brutal and mutilating, then the principles of complex thought will necessarily be principles of distinction, conjunction, and implication.

Join cause and effect, and the effect will come back on the cause through a feedback process, and the product will also be producer. You will distinguish these notions and you will join them at the same time. You will join One and the Many, you will unite them, but One will not dissolve in the Many, and the Many will continue to be part of the One. The principle of complexity, in a way, is founded on the predominance of complex conjunction. However, I profoundly believe that it is a cultural, historical task, profound and multiple. One can be the Saint John the Baptist of the paradigm of complexity and announce it is coming without being its Messiah.

4

COMPLEXITY AND ACTION[23]

ACTION IS ALSO A WAGER

Sometimes we have the impression that action simplifies, because with a choice, we decide, we close the matter. The example of an action that simplifies everything is Alexander's sword that cut through the Gordian knot that no one could undo with their fingers. Certainly, action is decision, a choice, but it is also a wager.

In this notion of wager, there is an awareness of risk and of uncertainty. Every strategy in any possible domain has this consciousness of the wager, and modern thought has understood that our most fundamental beliefs are the object of a wager. This is what Blaise Pascal told us about religious faith in the seventeenth century. We must be aware of our philosophical and political wagers.

Action is strategy. The word *strategy* does not mean a predetermined program we can apply *ne variatur* over time. Strategy permits, from an initial decision, to envisage a certain number of scenarios of action, scenarios that can be modified according to information arriving in the action and according to chance occurrences that will occur and disrupt the action.

Strategy battles against chance and seeks information. An army sends out scouts, that is to say, spies to find information, to eliminate a maximum of uncertainty. In addition, strategy does not limit itself to fighting against chance, but attempts to use it as well. Thus, the genius of Napoleon at Austerlitz was to use the meteorological chance event that placed a blanket of fog over the marshes that were already reputed to be impassable to soldiers. He created his strategy based on this fog, that allowed him to camouflage the movements of his army, and to take the most unprotected flank of the imperial army by surprise.

Strategy takes advantage of chance, and, when it is a strategy concerning another player, a good strategy uses the adversary's errors. In the game of football, the strategy consists of the balls involuntarily given up by the other team. The construction of the game is carried out by the deconstruction of the adversary's game. Finally the best strategy—if it benefits from a bit of luck—wins. Chance is not only a negative factor to reduce in the domain of strategy. It is also an opportunity to seize.

The problem of action should also make us aware of derailments and bifurcations: initial situations that are quite close can lead to gaps that cannot be remedied. Thus, when Martin Luther starts his movement, he thinks he is in agreement with the Church, and wants only to reform the abuses committed by the papacy in Germany. Then, from the moment when he has to decide either to renounce or to continue, he crosses the threshold from reformer to protester. An inexorable movement sweeps him away—as happens to all deviance— and it ends in a declaration of war, and the theses of Wittemberg (1517). The domain of action is very risky, very uncertain. It imposes on us a very keen awareness of risks, derailments, bifurcations, and imposes a reflection on complexity itself.

ACTION ESCAPES OUR INTENTIONS

This is where the notion of the ecology of action intervenes. As soon as an individual takes an action, whatever that action may be, it begins to escape from his intentions. The action enters into the universe of interactions and in the end, it is the environment that seizes it in the sense that it can become the opposite of the initial intention. Often the action will fly back at our heads like a boomerang. This obliges us to follow the action, to attempt to correct it—if there is still time—and sometimes to torpedo it like NASA engineers who, if a missile leaves its trajectory, send another missile to blow it up.

Action presupposes complexity, that is to say, risk, hazard, initiative, decision, awareness of derailments and transformations. The word *strategy* stands in opposition to the word *program*. For sequences situated in a stable environment, programs can be used. A program does not require vigilance. It doesn't require innovation. When we drive to work in our car, a part of our driving is programmed. If we hit an unexpected traffic jam, we have to then decide if we should change our route or not, and break the code; we need to use a strategy. This is why we must use multiple fragments of programmed action, to be able to concentrate on what is important, to strategize for risks.

There is not, on one side, a domain of complexity that includes thought and reflection, and on the other, a domain of simple things that includes action. Action is the concrete realm and is sometimes vital to complexity. Action can certainly be content with an immediate strategy that depends on intuition, the personal gifts of strategy. It would also benefit from complex thought, but complex thought is above all a challenge.

A simplified, linear vision has every chance to be mutilating. For example, the politics of oil took into consideration only the price factor without thinking of exhaustion of natural resources, the independent tendencies of the oil-producing countries, or political inconveniences. The experts pushed history, geography, sociology, politics, religion, mythology aside from their analysis, all of which have taken their revenge.

THE NON-TRIVIAL MACHINE

Human beings, society, enterprise—these are non-trivial machines. A trivial machine is one about which if you know all the inputs you know all the outputs. You can predict the behavior as soon as you know all that has gone into the machine. In a certain way, we are *also* trivial machines whose behavior can be largely predicted.

In fact, social life demands of us that we behave like trivial machines. Of course, we don't behave like pure automatons, we seek out non-trivial means as soon as we realize that we can reach our own objectives. What is important is that it is in moments of crisis, in moments of decisions, that the machine becomes non-trivial: it acts in a way that cannot be predicted. Everything that has to do with the emergence of the new is non-trivial and cannot be predicted. Thus, when students in China went to the streets by the thousands, China became a nontrivial machine. . . . In 1987–1989, in the Soviet Union, Gorbachev was behaving like a nontrivial machine! Everything that has happened in history, especially in times of crisis, are nontrivial events that cannot be predicted ahead of time. Joan of Arc, who heard voices and decided to go find the king of France, was behaving nontrivially. Everything of any importance that happens in France or in world politics has come out of the unexpected.

Our societies are nontrivial machines in the sense that they will incessantly know political, economical, and social crises. Every crisis is an increase in uncertainty. Predictability is reduced. Disorder becomes menacing. Antagonisms inhibit complementarities, virtual conflicts become actualized. Regulations fail or shatter. We must abandon programs, and invent new strategies to get out of the crisis. We must abandon solutions that have worked with past crises, and elaborate new solutions.

PREPARING FOR THE UNEXPECTED

Complexity is not a recipe for knowing the unexpected, but it does make us prudent and attentive. It does not let us fall asleep in the apparently mechanical and trivial determinism. It shows us that we should not believe that what is going on now will continue indefinitely. We may well know that everything that has happened of importance in world history or in our lives was totally unexpected, but we continue to act as if the unexpected will never again appear. To shake off this laziness of mind is a lesson of complex thought. Complex thought does not at all reject clarity, order, or determinism. It knows they are insufficient, it knows that we cannot program discovery, knowledge, or action.

Complexity needs a strategy. Certainly, programmed segments for sequences in which there is no randomness are useful or necessary. In normal situations automatic pilot is possible, but strategy is called for as soon as the unexpected or uncertainty arises, that is to say as soon as an important problem appears.

Simple thought solves simple problems without thought problems. Complex thought doesn't in itself resolve problems, but it constitutes an aid to a strategy that can resolve them. It says to us "help yourself, and complex thought will help you." What complex thought can do is to give everyone a memento, a reminder, that says, "Don't forget that reality is changing, don't forget that something new can (and will) spring up."

Complexity is situated at a point of departure for a richer, less mutilating action. I strongly believe that the less a thought is mutilating, the less it will mutilate human begins. We must remember the ravages that simplifying visions have caused, not only in the intellectual world, but in life. Much of the suffering of millions of beings results from the effects of fragmented and one-dimensional thought.

5

COMPLEXITY AND THE
ENTERPRISE[24]

Let's take a contemporary tapestry. It is made up of threads of linen, cotton, and wool, in various colors. To know this tapestry, it would be interesting to know the laws and the principles concerning each type of thread. However, the sum of knowledge of these types of thread used in the tapestry is insufficient for knowing the new reality that is the fabric, with the qualities and properties that are proper to this texture. It is also incapable of helping us know its form and its configuration.

In the first stage of complexity we have simple knowledge that does not help to know the properties of the whole. A banal observation that has consequences that are not banal; the tapestry is more than the sum of the threads that make it up. A whole is more than the sum of the parts.

In the second stage of complexity, the fact that there is a tapestry means that the qualities of this or that type of thread cannot all be fully expressed. They are inhibited or virtualized. The whole is, therefore, less than the sum of its parts.

The third stage of complexity poses problems for our capacity to understand, and for our mental structure. The whole is at the same time more and less than the sum of its parts.

In this tapestry, as in an organization, the threads are not placed randomly. They are organized based on a canvas, on a synthetic unity where each part works together with the whole. The tapestry itself is a perceptible and knowable phenomenon that cannot be explained by any simple law.

THREE CAUSALITIES

An organization such as an enterprise is situated in the marketplace. It produces objects or services, things that become exterior to it and enter into the world of consumption. To limit oneself to a heteroproductive vision of the enterprise would be insufficient, because by producing things and services the enterprise also produces itself. This means that it produces all the elements necessary to its own survival and its own organization. In organizing production of objects and services, it organizes itself, it maintains itself, if necessary it repairs itself, if things go well it develops itself as it develops its production.

Thus in producing products that are independent of the producer, a process develops by which the producer produces itself. On the one hand, its self-production is necessary to the production of objects, and on the other hand, the production of objects is necessary to its self-production.

Complexity appears in this statement: Things are produced at the same time we self-produce; the producer itself is its own product.

This statement creates a few problems of causality.

First, linear causality: If with some raw material, applying some process of transformation, we produce some consumer object, we are in a frame of linear causality: x cause produces y effects.

Second, feedback loop causality: An enterprise needs to be regulated. It must carry out its production based on external needs, from the power of its work and its internal energy capacity. But we know—have known for about 40 years now, thanks to cybernetics—that the effect (sales or slumps) can feed back to stimulate or slow the production of objects and services in the enterprise.

Third, recursive causality: In the recursive process, the effects and products are necessary to the process that creates them. The product is producer of that which produces it.

These three causalities are found at all levels of complex organizations. Society, for example, is produced by the interactions between the people that make it up. Society itself, as an organized and organizing whole, feeds back to produce the individuals through education, language, and school. The individuals, in their interactions, produce society, which produces the individuals that produce it. This creates a spiral circuit through historical evolution.

This understanding of complexity requires a relatively deep change in our mental structures. The risk, if this change of mental structures were not to take place, would be to direct us toward pure confusion or the denial of problems. There are not, on the one side, individuals, and, on the other, society; on one side species, and on the other individuals, on one side the enterprise, with its plan, its production program, its marketing study, and on the other, its problems with human relations, personnel, public relations. The two processes are inseparable and interdependent.

FROM SELF-ORGANIZATION
TO SELF-ECO-ORGANIZATION

The enterprise, the living organism, self-organizes and produces itself. At the same time, it carries out self-eco-organizing and self-eco-production. This complex concept deserves elucidating.

The enterprise is situated in an exterior environment that is in turn integrated in a eco-organized system or ecosystem. Let's take the example of plants or animals: their chronobiological processes know the cycle of day and night as well as the cycle of the seasons. Cosmic order is, in a way, integrated in the interior of the organization of living species.

Let's look at this further, through an experiment carried out in 1951 in the planetarium at Bremen on a migrating bird, the warbler. The planetarium projected the sky and constellations from Germany to Egypt in front of the bird's eyes because it migrates toward the valley of the Nile in winter. In the planetarium, the bird followed the map of the sky without fail, and stopped under the sky of Luxor. It thus "computed" its itinerary based on celestial milestones. This experience proves that the warbler had, in a manner of speaking, the sky in its head.

We human beings know the world through the messages that our senses transmit to our brains. The world is present inside our minds, which are inside the world.

The principle of self-eco-organization has a holographic value. As the holographic image is linked to the fact that each point possesses the quasi totality of the information about the whole, so, in a certain manner, the whole as a whole of which we are a part is present in our minds. Simplified vision would be to say that the part is in the whole. Complex vision says that not only is the part in the whole; the whole is in the part that is inside the whole! This complexity is something other than the confusion of the whole in the whole and vice versa.

This is true of each cell of our organism that contains the totality of the genetic code present in our bodies. This is true of society: from childhood, society imprints itself in our minds, through education in families, schools, and universities.

We are facing extremely complex systems where the part is in the whole and the whole is in the part. This is true of the enterprise with its rules of functioning and within which the laws of an entire society are in play.

TO LIVE AND MAKE A DEAL
WITH DISORDER

An enterprise self-eco-organizes in its market, which market is a phenomenon that is at once ordered, organized, and random. It is random because there is no absolute certainty about the opportunities and possibilities of selling products and services, even if there are possibilities, probabilities, and plausibilities. The market is a mixture of order and disorder.

Unhappily—or happily—the entire universe is a cocktail of order, disorder, and organization. We are in a universe from which we cannot exclude risk, uncertainty, and disorder. We have to live and deal with disorder.

Order refers to everything that is repetition, constant, invariant, everything that can be put under the aegis of a highly probable relation, framed within the dependence of a law.

Disorder refers to everything that is irregularity, deviation as regards a given structure, random, unpredictability.

In a universe of pure order, there would be no innovation, no creation, no evolution. There would be no life or human existence. But neither would any existence be possible in pure disorder, because there would be no element of stability on which to found an organization.

Organizations need order and they need disorder. In a universe in which systems submit to growth of disorder and tend to disintegrate, their organization allows them to drive back, capture, and use disorder.

Every organization, like every physical, organizational, and, of course, living phenomenon, tends to degrade and degenerate. The phenomenon of disintegration and decadence is a normal phenomenon. In other words, what is normal is not that things last as they are, which would, on the contrary, be worrisome. There is no recipe for equilibrium. The only way to fight against degeneration is permanent regeneration, in other words, the aptitude of the whole of the organization to regenerate, and to organize itself by facing all disintegrating processes.

STRATEGY, PROGRAM, AND ORGANIZATION

Order, disorder, program, strategy!

The notion of strategy is in opposition to the notion of program.

A program is a sequence of predetermined actions that must function in circumstances that allow their completion. If the external circumstances are unfavorable, the program stops or fails. As we saw earlier, strategy, on the other hand, elaborates one or several scenarios. From the beginning, strategy prepares itself, if there is anything new or unexpected, to integrate, modify, or enrich its action.

The advantage of a program is obviously a great economy: we don't have to think, everything is done automatically. A strategy, on the contrary, is determined by taking account of a random situation, adverse or even adversarial elements, and it is brought to modify itself depending on information furnished en route, it can have a great deal of flexibility. But a strategy, in order for it to be carried out by an organization, requires that the organization not be conceived to obey a program, but that it can work with elements capable of contributing to the elaboration and development of the strategy.

I believe, therefore, that our ideal model of functionality and rationality is not only an abstract model, it is also a harmful model. It is harmful for those who are in administration and in fact, for the whole of social life. Such a model is obviously rigid, and everything that is programmed suffers from rigidity in comparison with strategy. Of course, from an administrative perspective we cannot say that everyone should become a strategist because that would result in total disorder. However, in general, the problems of rigidity and the development of possibilities and "adaptability" is avoided, which favors sclerosis in the bureaucratic phenomenon.

Bureaucracy is ambivalent. Bureaucracy is rational because it applies to impersonal rules that apply to everyone, and it ensures cohesion and functionality in an organization. On the other hand, bureaucracy can be criticized as a pure instrument of decisions that aren't necessarily rational. Bureaucracy can be considered a parasitic totality in which several blockages and bottlenecks develop. It can become a parasitic phenomenon in the heart of society.

We can, therefore, consider the problem of bureaucracy under this double parasitic and rational angle, and it is a shame that sociological thought has not jumped the hurdle of this alternative. Without a doubt, sociology has not jumped it because the problem of bureaucracy and administration must first be formulated in fundamental terms at the level of complexity.

The vice of the Tayloristic conception of work was that it considered humans only as physical machines. Then we realized that humans were also biological: we adapted biological humans to their work and the working conditions to the humans; Then, when we realized that there were also psychological humans, who where frustrated by these fractured tasks, we invented job enrichment. The evolution of work illustrates the passage from one-dimensionality to multidimensionality. We are only at the beginning of this process.

The factor of play is a factor of disorder but also of flexibility: imposing an unshakable order within an enterprise is not efficient. All instructions that require, the immediate shut down of the sector or the machine in the event of breakdown of unexpected incident are counter-efficient. Some initiative must be left to each level and to each individual.

COMPLEMENTARY AND ANTAGONISTIC RELATIONS

Relations inside an organization, a society, an enterprise, are complementary and antagonistic at the same time. This antagonistic complementarity is founded on an extraordinary ambiguity. Daniel Mothé, once a professional worker at Renault, describes how in his division an informal, secret, clandestine association took shape against the rigid organization of work, permitting workers to gain a bit of personal autonomy and freedom. This secret organization created a flexible organization of work. The resistance was collaborative, and through it, things worked.

This example can be extended to multiple domains, for example, to the concentration camp at Buchenwald, created in 1933 for political and regular

German prisoners. In the beginning, the regular prisoners had jobs as Kapos and minor responsibilities in accounting, in the kitchen. The political prisoners made it clear that they could make things work better, without misappropriation or loss. The SS entrusted the communist political prisoners with the care of this organization. In this way a communist organization collaborated with the SS while fighting against it. The victory of the allies and the liberation of the camp turned this collaboration into a form of resistance.

Let's take the case of the Soviet economy until 1990. It was regulated, in principle, by central planning, which was hyperrigid, hypermeticulous, and so forth. The extremely strict, programmed, imperative character of this planning made it inapplicable. It worked, through a lot of negligence because there was cheating and wangling at every level. For example, directors of enterprises called each other to exchange products. This meant that at the top there were rigid orders, but at the bottom there was spontaneous organizing anarchy. Frequent absenteeism was necessary because the work conditions were such that people had to be absent to find other small odd jobs to complement their salaries. This spontaneous anarchy expressed the population's resistance to and collaboration with the system that oppressed it.

In other words, the economy of the USSR worked because of this spontaneously anarchic response on the part of individuals to anonymous orders from on high, and, of course, there must have been elements of coercion for it to work. However, it did not work only because there were police. It worked also because there was a tolerance of what was happening at the base, and this tolerance ensured the functioning of an absurd machine that otherwise could not have functioned.

In fact, the system did not fall apart. It was a political decision that led to its abandonment because of its enormous waste, its weak performance, its lack of inventiveness. While it lasted, it was spontaneous anarchy that made programmed planning function. It was resistance within the machine that made the machine work.

Disorder constitutes the inevitable, necessary, and often fecund response to the sclerotic, schematic, abstract, and simplifying character of order.

A global historical problem is, therefore, posed: How to integrate into enterprises the freedom and disorder that can bring adaptiveness and inventiveness but can also bring decomposition and death.

THE NECESSITY FOR A LIVED SOLIDARITY

There is, therefore, an ambiguity of battle, of resistance, of collaboration, of antagonism, and complementarity necessary to organizational complexity. The problem rests on an excess of complexity, which, in the end, is destructuring.

One can say loosely that the more an organization is complex, the more it tolerates disorder. This gives it a certain vitality because the individuals are apt to take initiatives to fix this or that problem without having to go through a central hierarchy. It is a more intelligent way to respond to certain challenges from the outside. However, an excess of complexity ends up destructuring. To a certain extent, an organization that has only freedom and very little order, would disintegrate unless it had, in addition to this freedom, a deep solidarity between its members. Lived solidarity is the only thing that allows an increase in complexity. In the end, informal networks, collaborative resistances, autonomy, disorder are the necessary ingredients for the vitality of enterprises.

This can open a world of reflections. Thus the atomization of our society requires new solidarity spontaneously lived and not imposed by the law, like social security.

6

ON THE NOTION OF THE SUBJECT

Translated by Sean M. Kelly

I

There is considerable controversy surrounding the notion of the subject. It is a paradoxical notion which is at once self-evident and problematic. At first glance, its meaning appears quite obvious, even banal, because the first person singular exists in almost every language. It seems equally self-evident to philosophical reflection since, as Descartes so clearly demonstrated, though I may doubt, I cannot doubt that I am doubting, and therefore that I am thinking, which is to say that it is I who am thinking. It is at this level of reflection that the subject makes its appearance.

Nevertheless, the notion of the subject is not so obvious as all that—for where exactly is this subject? What is it? What is it founded upon? Is the subject a mere illusion or something fundamental? It can, of course, appear in the form of the supreme reality. Thus, when the Eternal appears to Moses and the latter asks, "But who then are You?" the Eternal responds: "I am who I am." Or in another rendering: "I am the one who Is." In other words, God appears in the form of absolute subject!

In many philosophies and metaphysics, the subject coincides with the soul, with the divine, or at least the superior part of ourselves, because it is here that we find discernment, freedom, the moral will, etc. However, if we consider the matter from another angle, that of the sciences, for example, all that we see is physical, biological, sociological, or cultural determinism and from this perspective, the subject seems to dissolve.

Now, in our Western culture, ever since the 17th century, we have suffered from a strange schizophrenic disjunction: in our daily lives, we feel ourselves to be subjects and we see others in this way. We say, for instance," What a brave man!", "What a wonderful person! Or perhaps, "What a rogue!" or "That bastard!" We say such things to try to capture something of the way people strike us as subjects. But if we examine these same people, and ourselves, from the point of view of determinism, their subjectivity once again dissolves and vanishes. This disjunction is the result of a deeply-rooted cultural paradigm, a paradigm which Descartes helped to formulate and which he merely expressed in his own fashion rather than invented. What Descartes saw was that there are two worlds: a world constituted by objective, scientific knowledge—the world of objects—and a world constituted by an intuitive, reflexive knowledge—the world of subjects. On the one hand, the world of the soul, spirit, feeling, philosophy, and literature, and on the other, the world of the sciences, technology, and mathematics. We are still split between these two worlds. What this means is that we cannot find the least support for the notion of the subject in classical science. By contrast, as soon as we leave the scientific domain and undertake the kind of reflection evident in Descartes' Cogito, the subject becomes the ground of truth, of any possible truth. In this way we are led to the idea of the transcendental Ego as formulated by Kant.

For classical science, subjectivity appears as something contingent and the source of errors (in terms of the science of information, it is equated with the "noise" that must be completely filtered out). It is for this reason, moreover, that classical science has always excluded the observer from the act of observation and the conceiver from the act of conceiving, as though, practically speaking, the subject did not really exist or, on the contrary, was firmly seated on the throne of absolute truth.

The 20th Century saw the invasion by classical science of the hitherto separate domains of the humanities and social sciences. The subject was eliminated from psychology and replaced by stimuli, responses, and behaviors. The subject was eliminated from history, which no longer concerned itself with personalities and their decisions, but only with social determinants. The subject was eliminated from anthropology, which now saw only structures. The same can be said for sociology. One could even say that, at various times and each in their own way, Levi-Strauss, Althusser, and Lacan (to name some of the most prominent figures) at once liquidated the notion of the human being and that of the subject, in this way inverting Freud's famous maxim: "Where It (das Es) was, 'I' have become." From the structuralist and scientistic perspective, the "I" must be liquidated and replaced by "It." Still, there has been a certain (usually belated) return of the subject, as with Foucault or Barthes, coinciding with a return of Eros and of literature.

In philosophical circles, however, the notion of the subject has once again become problematical. What, or who, is the subject? Must we really come to know and acknowledge it? Or is it a mere epiphenomenon or an illusion? I would answer with the following proposition: I believe in the possibility of a scientific, rather than a metaphysical, grounding for the notion of the subject, one which involves what I call a "biological" definition of the term in question, though not in the sense of contemporary biological discourse. I could say biological, by which I mean corresponding to the very logic of living beings. And why are we now able to conceive of the notion of the subject in a scientific manner? To begin with, because it is possible to reconceptualize the notion of autonomy, something which was impossible within a mechanistic and deterministic world view.

This notion of autonomy does not correspond to the old notion of freedom, which was to a certain extent immaterial and detached from constraints and physical contingencies. It is, on the contrary, a notion closely linked to that of dependence, and the latter is inseparable from the notion of self-organization. In a short and masterful piece written in 1968, Heinz Von Foerster indicated the paradox of self-organization from the outset. "Though self-organization obviously signifies autonomy," he wrote, "a self-organizing system is a system which must work to construct and reconstruct its autonomy, and this requires energy." By virtue of the second law of thermodynamics, the system must draw energy from outside; to be autonomous, therefore, it must be dependent on the outside world. And we know from observation that this dependence is not merely energetic, but informational, since living beings extract information from the outside world in organizing their behavior. What's more, the system draws organization from the outside world, something which Schroedinger already pointed out. Thus, for example, we have encoded within us, as organisms, the chronological organization of the Earth's rotation around the sun. As with many animals and plants, we have a rhythm of approximately 24 hours, which we call circadian. Our biological clock has internalized the alternation of night and day. Our societies, moreover, require a calendar that is set to the movements of sun and moon to organize our collective lives. Autonomy, therefore, involves a profound energetic, informational, and organizational dependence with respect to the outside world; it is for these reasons that I use the term self-eco-organization, rather than simply self-organization, in recognition of Von Foerster's principle whereby self-organization is itself dependent.

It is possible to conceive of a certain autonomy at the level of artificial machines. A central heating system, for example, has, through its feedback mechanism, a thermal autonomy, which allows it to maintain a constant temperature, whatever the outside conditions. A living organism, for its part, has a richer and much more complex system of regulation, one that allows for homeostasis, which is to say a certain constancy of temperature, of pH levels, and of all the elements that constitute its internal environment. However, there is a great difference between the living organism and those artificial machines which possess a certain regulative autonomy, for the latter is obviously dependent not only on energy, on the fuel supplied from outside, but also on the human engineer who repairs the machine when it breaks down. Living machines, by contrast, have the ability constantly to repair and regenerate themselves. They can do this because they possess what I have called recursive organization, an organization where the effects and the products themselves become causal and productive within the organizational cycle. Such, then, are some of the conceptual elements necessary to understand the notion of autonomy, and particularly so when it is a question of living organization.

II

At this point we have to consider a second notion which, though in itself long familiar, has. Taken on new dimensions—namely, that of the individual. For several centuries, biology had understood very well that there existed some kind of relation between the species and the individual. The typical way of conceiving of this relation was to see the species as a kind of general pattern or model, with individuals as its particular exemplars. But there was another way of seeing things, which consisted in saying: "But species don't exist! One never sees a species. One sees individuals, but never species." It has been the case that, according to the perspective adopted, either the species disappears and the individual occupies the whole of our conceptual field or, on the contrary, the individual disappears, becomes something contingent or ephemeral and it is the species which abides through time and possesses the true reality. One or the other of these perspectives has tended to dominate, whereas at bottom it is a question of coming to terms with the paradoxical quality of the relation in question.

One sees the same paradox at the level of micro-physics the relation between particles and waves. Niels Bohr observed that, depending on the experimental conditions, the same quantum of energy could manifest itself either as a particle—that is to say as a discrete, limited, material body—or as a wave—something immaterial and continuous. Despite the logical contradiction between these two terms, empirically, it is one or the other which manifests according to the conditions of observation. Niels Bohr himself remarked that "these two terms, though logically exclusive, remain complementary." There is a similar complementarity between the individual and the species, albeit one less paradoxical in nature. Why is this? Because we must conceive the relation between individual and species in light of the recursive processes to which I have already alluded. The individual is obviously a product; it is the product, as is the case with all sexually differentiated beings, of the meeting between sperm and egg, which is to say a process of reproduction. But this product is itself productive with respect to its offspring. We are both products and producers in the cycle of life. Similarly, society is incontestably the product of interactions among individuals. These interactions, however, create an organization which possesses its own qualities, notably language and culture. And these same qualities retroact on the individuals from the moment of birth, to ensure that they acquire language, culture, etc. . . . . This means that individuals produce society, which in turn produces individuals. We have to think in this way in order to grasp the paradoxical relation involved. Thus, the individual is an uncertain object. In effect, from a certain angle, the individual is everything; without it, there is nothing. But from another angle, it is nothing or is eclipsed. From being a producer, it becomes a product; from cause it becomes effect, and vice versa. We can thus understand the autonomy of the individual, but in a manner that is extremely relativized and complex.

III

With this we come to the notion of the subject—and more particularly to that of the individual-subject. This notion clearly implies both autonomy and dependence. In other words, the definition of the subject presupposes the autonomy-dependence of the individual, without, however, being reduced to it. For there is something more involved. But to understand this something more, it is necessary to grasp, in a fundamental way, the nature of living organization. While molecular biology and genetics have given us all the elements required to understand this organization, they have nothing to say regarding the nature of organization itself. This is one of the basic deficiencies of biology, though it should come as no surprise. We know, for example, that physics, which made remarkable discoveries in the last century, did so with the limited idea (incredible today) that the universe was totally deterministic and mechanist. And yet as early as the beginning of the 19th Century, the second principle of thermodynamics had already been formulated, and with it, disorder had been introduced into this same universe.

In its preoccupation with identifying molecules, genes, macromolecules, and particular processes, molecular biology has forgotten completely about the problem of the self-eco-organization of the living being. In fact, however, the study of genes and RNA has revealed something that could be assimilated to the notions of information, program, and memory—which is to say, to something of a cognitive nature. And this cognitive something plays a permanent role in all processes of living organization. It is the links between DNA—RNA—proteins which control the production of molecules and which inhibit this production, thereby regenerating the molecules which degenerate. It is these processes which control the behavior of bacteria and which command the autoreproduction of unicellular organisms. It is these processes which allow for reorganization, repair, and activity in general.

If we take the case of the least complex (it would be inappropriate to say the most simple) form of living organization—bacterial organization—we see that the bacterium is at once, and indissociably, a being, a machine, and a computer. In the case of our artificial machines, by contrast, we have the controlling computer, on the one hand, and the machine to which it is connected, on the other. With the bacterium, we have neither a computer nor a machine by itself, but both at once in the same thing. We have a being, a machine-being which is a computing being. I use the word "computing" rather than "calculating," which has too much of an arithmetical ring (despite the fact that the word is used non-arithmetically, as in the logical calculus of propositions). It is a computing being, I say, which means that it processes signs and data about its internal and external environments. Here we see at the same time an analogy but especially a great difference with respect to the computation of artificial computers. Not only because it is not simply a question here of binary processing, but of a more complex, and more analogical mode of processing which remains a mystery; but also in that this difference resides in the fact that the bacterium computes from itself, by itself, and for itself, which is to say that it is animated by a kind of auto-finality; it constitutes itself by-and-for-itself, in a manner reminiscent of Hegel's use of the term "*für sich*." This is what I call the *computo*. The Cartesian *cogito* appears much later, as it requires a well developed brain, as well as language and culture. The computo is necessary to the existence of the being and of the subject. The bacterium might say "*computo ergo sum.*" I compute, therefore I am. And why is this? Because if it stops computing, it dies, for it can no longer produce the elements of which it is constituted. Thus, in looking at a bacterium under the microscope, it answers with a continuous "*computo ergo sum.*" One has to know how to listen. But what could it mean to say, "I compute for myself?" It means that I place myself at the center of the world, the center of my world, the world that I know, to process it, to consider it, and accomplish all the measures of protection, defense, etc. It is here that the notion of the subject makes its appearance, along with the *computo* and its egocentrism. The notion of the subject is indissociable from this act of computation, where one is not only one's own finality, but where one also constitutes one's own identity.

IV

We must now consider the basis of this principle of identity which, from the start, already appears complex, since it is not readily assimilable to the Aristotelian principle of identity. This principle, which is presupposed by the act of computation, and without which there would be no *computo*, is a principle of difference and equivalence, which I would formulate thus: "I am me!" But just what is this "I"? It is the occupying of an egocentric site. "I" Really means: "I occupy an egocentric site. I speak." "Me" for its part, is precisely the objectification of the I. Thus: "I am me" means that the "me" is not exactly the same as the I, since, in the act wherein the me is formed, the me appears different—it is objectified—whereas the I is the pure uprising of the subject. The act which simultaneously posits the difference between the I and the me along with their identity allows for the *computo* to process the being as subject. Thus the bacterium can process its molecules in an objective manner while remaining a being which is animated by its self-organizational subjectivity. And I would add that the me, as the objectification of the individual-subject, reflects the self, which is the physical entity. The self includes the me and the I.

There is, in effect, a complex game enacted between these terms which are at once identical and different: "me, myself, and I." Obviously, I am expressing all of this in human language, of which the bacterium is completely ignorant. The bacterium, however, contains a kind of software, whose principle—"I Am me"—allows it to process itself, and without which it could not exist.

There is thus a principle of complex identity which allows for all operations dealing with the objective processing of molecules, cells, and actions undertaken by a polycellular organism. The process is objective but with a subjective finality. It is in this way that the principle makes self-reference possible: I can process myself, refer to myself, because I need a minimum of self objectification though I remain an I-subject. However, just as self-organization is in fact self-eco-organization, self-reference is really self-exo-reference, which is to say that to refer to oneself, one must refer to the outside world. There is a fundamental distinction made between self and not-self. And this fundamental distinction is not merely cognitive, but valuative as well: value is attributed to the self and non-value to the not-self. It is this process which is constitutive of subjective identity. Such is the manner in which the distinctions between self/not-self, me/not-me, and between the "I" and "other I"'s are established. Science's recognition of the distinction between self and not-self emerged toward the end of the Sixties within a particular branch of biology: immunology. The immune system, which protects us from external threats, is a system which, thanks to a kind of molecular ID card specific to each organism, allows for the recognition of everything that belongs to the self. Whatever corresponds to the ID card is accepted, and whatever doesn't correspond is rejected, depending on the degree of vitality of the system in question, of course. To be sure, there is the possibility of error because, as soon as one enters the world of information and cognition, we simultaneously enter the world of error. For instance, errors arise in the case of viruses that possess the same molecular patterns of identity as the host organism, in a manner reminiscent of enemy soldiers disguised in our uniforms so as to enter our strongholds and conquer them from within.

We thus have a system based on the difference between self and not-self, along with the value attributed to the protection of self and the rejection of the not-self. Now, even prior to the existence of the kind of well-differentiated immune system we find in the higher animals, uni-cellular organisms distinguish between self and not-self. When, for instance, they absorb nutrients from outside, what they assimilate becomes part of the self and what is rejected as non-assimilable becomes waste (urine and excrement with more evolved beings).

It is in this way that, step by step, we can start making sense of the notion of the subject. It is no easy task, since it requires the prior elaboration of the principle of the *computo* along with what might be called the "software" behind the principle of identity.

There is a second, and quite fascinating, principle of identity which maintains the invariance of the I-subject despite the extraordinary modifications constantly taking place at the physical, molecular, and cellular level. This is apparent not only in the fact that, every four years, the greater part of the cells that make up my organism have disappeared to be replaced by others—which is to say that, biologically speaking, I am no longer the same being that I was four years ago. There are also enormous changes which accompany the shifts from childhood through adolescence to old age. And yet, when I look at a childhood photograph of myself, I say: "That's me!" And yet, I am no longer that child, and I no longer have that body or that face. But the occupation of this central site of the I, which abides throughout all these changes, establishes the continuity of identity. We even live in the illusion of possessing a stable identity, without really being aware of how different we are according to our moods—whether we are angry, loving, or hating—and due to the fact (but this is a whole other story) that we are all double, triple, and multiple personalities. It is the I which brings about the unity. Such is the second principle of identity.

V

There is something more to the elementary notion of the subject, because I have not yet come to the human subject, though everything I have to say obviously applies to human subjects as well.

There are two associated subjective principles: the principle of exclusion and that of inclusion. What is the principle of exclusion? Linguists have noted that anyone can say "I," but that no one can say it for me. The "I", in other words, is something totally banal, and at the same time something absolutely unique. And this is true even in the case of identical or homozygotic, twins who have exactly the same genetic make-up. To be sure, such twins share a particular complicity, but neither can say "I" in the other's place. More remarkable still, there are snakes from the California desert at the San Diego zoo which, as a result of a genetic accident, have two heads per single organism. This is a quite complicated case, as they possess a single immune system and a single organismic subjectivity, at least until the two heads become separated. There are, however, undeniably two subjects from the cerebral point of view. What's more, this proves to be a fatal arrangement! And why? Because each head looks out for its own food, which means that when one head finds food, the other pushes it aside, and so these poor two-headed snakes succeed only with great difficulty in finding enough to eat and can only survive in zoos where each head is fed separately. Thus we see that the principle of exclusion is at work even in the case of two snake-heads sharing the same body.

But this principle of exclusion is inseparable from a principle of inclusion which makes it possible for us to integrate other selves within our subjectivity, we can integrate our personal subjectivity within a more collective subjectivity—within a "we." Our offspring and parents, for example, are part of this circle of inclusion. They are part of us, and we of them, subjectively. And there are often conflicts between the two principles. We see the conflict in animals when, for instance, we are surprised to see lionesses devour their cubs. It is sometimes the case in the animal world that parents, who are otherwise so concerned about their offspring, sometimes eat them. On the one hand, they sacrifice themselves for their offspring in trying to protect them against aggressors, and on the other hand, if they see that there is not enough food, they eat them. There is thus this ambivalence between the principles of exclusion and inclusion. This ambivalence is quite pronounced, if variable, in our own case with respect to those close to us, those to whom we are subjective-ly linked.

The same thing happens with one's country in times of threat or danger. This society, which we inhabit in an egoistic and egocentric manner, to which we are bound by self-interest, finds itself in danger and we are suddenly swept up by a communitarian wave into a "we." We are brothers and sisters, children of the nation which becomes our mother, and the State our father. But some escape the wave and say, "I want to save my own life", and they desert. Here, too, then, there is a struggle between the principle of inclusion and that of exclusion. Thus the subject—and especially the human subject—can oscillate between an absolute egocentrism, where exclusion dominates, and self sacrific-ing devotion.

And there are other quite murky, complex, and fascinating cases. There is a book by Jaynes, *The Origins of Consciousness in the Breakdown of the Bicameral Mind*. I don't know whether or not his thesis is valid, though it seems to me to illustrate something that may be valid. In the empires of the ancient world, such as the Egyptian or the Assyrian, ruled by the king and his priests, there were two chambers in the minds of the individual-subjects (the latter, not being citizens, lived in a state of subjugation). In one of these chambers resides the dictates of the State, the power which commands: "Do this! Obey!" Like an automaton, the individual obeys the injunction from on high. The other cham-ber is devoted to domestic life, to one's children, and to daily concerns. And these two chambers do not communicate. In the Greek islands, however, in Athens, with the rise of the citizen and democracy, the two chambers will start to communicate, which means that the subject will be able to keep an eye on power, on the State and the gods. We too, to a certain extent, have these two chambers, and the air often circulates between them. I give this as an illustra-tion of how the principles of inclusion and exclusion can be combined.

To these two principles we must add a third—the principle of intercom-munication with what is similar, with what is like oneself, a principle which fol-lows in a sense from the principle of inclusion. We see it already with bacteria. A phenomenon has been observed which at first was considered a manifesta-tion of the sexuality of bacteria: a bacterium would approach another and, at that moment, would produce a kind of canal or peduncle which allowed it to penetrate its sister bacterium and inject a little DNA. One suspects this gift of DNA has some utilitarian purpose. According to one of the hypotheses formu-lated, when the bacteria are attacked by antibiotics and many of them die, a few manage to develop resistances thanks to their sisters' injection of DNA which serves as a defense. While this problem is really beyond the scope of this essay, I wanted to express my admiration for this act which, I would say, is at once pre-sexual and post-sexual, an act which involves both more and less than sex-uality. Would that we, too, could be like these bacteria and give such a gift as an expression of our love!

It has recently been discovered that there is communication between trees of the same species. The discovery followed the experiment of a group of sadistic scientists (as they must sometimes be to do experimental work!) who removed all the leaves from a tree to see how it would behave. The tree reacted as expected, that is by increasing its secretion of sap in order to replace the leaves that had been removed. The tree also secreted a certain substance which protects it from parasites. The tree knew full well that it had been attacked by a parasite, but the poor thing thought the parasite was an insect. It did not understand that it was the greatest of parasites—human beings. What's interesting, however, is that the neighboring trees of the same species started secreting the same antiparasitic substance as the tree that had been attacked.

Thus, intercommunication exists in the world of unicellular organisms, in the plant world and, it goes without saying, in the animal world. With human beings, we have the peculiar situation, linked to the dialectical game between the principles of inclusion and exclusion, of having much communication and much non-communication! But at least we have the possibility of communicating about our lack of communication, which means, as well, that the problem of communication becomes much more complex.

VI

One can define the subject as a fundamental quality proper to living beings, a quality which cannot be reduced to morphological or psychological singularity since, as we saw above, two psychologically and morphologically identical twins are still two distinct subjects. It is a quality that involves the overlapping of multiple elements. What's more, as the individual lives in a world where there is randomness, uncertainty, danger, and mortality, the subject inevitably possesses an existential character. It carries within itself the fragility and uncertainty of existence from birth to death. It is a poor little *Dasein*, as Heidegger might say.

Everything human is subject to the characteristics I have just expressed, without, however, being reduced to them. There is something more, much more. To begin with, there is our neuro-cerebral apparatus. We don't have a monopoly here, as this apparatus evolved along with the vertebrates, mammals, primates, hominids, etc. This apparatus obviously controls both knowing and behavior, by linking them both together. And it is here that we see a different level of subjectivity than that of the immune system, though both levels remain, of course, in communication. This is to say that we have to do here with a cerebral subject which constitutes itself as subject in the "very act of perception, of representation, decision, and behavior. And we have become aware that, in the animal world, and especially with mammals, affectivity has developed along with this cerebral apparatus: affectivity appears to many of us as the single most characteristic trait of the subject (since, when we say, "It's subjective," we allude to something linked to emotions and feelings, and always with an element of the contingent and arbitrary). The development of affectivity is linked to the superior development of the subject. Add to this the fact that in the animal world, in the world of mammals and primates, the development of affectivity neither runs contrary to intelligence nor inhibits its development. The two are narrowly linked. For we human beings, this means that the affective character of our subjectivity will forever be with us; but it is not alone, for it is linked to those egocentric and altruistic characteristics I have already talked about.

There is a second property which is truly specific to the human subject, as it is linked to language and culture. With the latter, the subject can become self-conscious by means of language as its instrument of objectification. Here we see a consciousness of being conscious and of being conscious of the self in a manner that is clearly inseparable from the notions of self-reference and reflexivity. It is in consciousness that we objectify ourselves, only to re-subjectify ourselves in an ongoing loop. We have surpassed the bacterium in its processes of objectification and re-subjectification. What's more, in all instances of archaic humanity, as I sought to demonstrate in *L'homme et la mort*, the presence of the "double" is a manifestation of the same impetus to subjective objectification proper to the human subject. This double—a corporeal specter which is perceived as identical to the self—is at once *alter-ego* and *ego-alter*. It manifests itself in shadows, reflections, and dreams, since we know that, while we dream, lying in bed, we are also wandering about and involved in all kinds of adventures. And with the coming of death, the double detaches itself from the body and goes on living its life. This experience of the double is the archaic form of the experience of the subject's self objectification, and only once we succeed in interiorizing it does it become the "soul" or "spirit." We have, then, this second, self-conscious level of subjective being, and with it, we also have freedom.

Freedom. Here again we find a concept which we can pull from its self-validating perch in the metaphysical heavens, setting it in the context of distinctly living and human organization with its dependencies and constraints. Freedom can be defined as the possibility of choice between diverse alternatives. Freedom also presupposes two conditions. To begin with, there is an internal condition, involving the cerebral, mental, and intellectual ability to consider a situation and establish choices and chances of success. Then there are external conditions which render the choices possible. Obviously, if one is in prison, one might preserve a good amount of mental or internal freedom, but one cannot chose where to go on vacation, where to practice one's profession, etc. In this way we can observe different types and degrees of freedom according to the breadth and depth of our choices.

Finally, there is that place within our human subjectivity which is inhabited by the notions of soul and spirit (animus–anima), and we have this deep feeling of incompleteness at the level of soul, an incompleteness which can only be healed by another subject. And it is, at bottom, in loving relationships, with the feeling of being in love, that we have the idea that the other restores to us the wholeness of our soul, even as they remain wholly other to us. They are us as much as they are other. We thus have these two levels of subjectivity, and while many have often sought the foundation of the notion of the subject in these specifically human traits, they could not, however, manifest themselves were it not for the prior, biological level of the subject. One cannot, moreover, reduce subjectivity to any of its elements, whether it be affectivity, contingency, or consciousness.

In other words, when Descartes says: "*cogito ergo sum*"—I think, therefore I am—he in fact implies the following operation: "I think" is a reflexive assertion which means: I think that I think." In this assertion, the I objectifies itself in an implicit "me," "I think myself," "I think myself thinking." In so doing, Descartes unconsciously effects the elementary computational operation, "I am me," he discovers that this "me" which thinks is a subject "I" Am. If the cogitating subject were to say, "Ah! Therefore I exist!", it would seem a pedestrian truth, since one could reply: "But all I have to do is pinch you to show that you exist." There are a thousand ways to prove that one exists. What's interesting here is this ergo: "I cannot doubt that I am a subject." But what Descartes did implies the computo. His cogito presupposes the *computo*.

One should not lose sight of the fact that our *cogitos*, that is to say our consciousness as subjects, depend upon the fundamental *computo* which the billions of our brain cells, in their organizational and creative interactions, incessantly cause to emerge. In other words, there is no *cogito* without the *computo*. It is precisely our consciousness which brings us face to face with the tragedy of subjectivity, something of which the bacterium is not conscious (at least so far as we can at present tell, for we have often underestimated the intellectual capacities of other living beings). In the absence of further evidence, it would appear that the bacterium does not possess consciousness as we experience it, as this consciousness requires a well-developed brain along with language and culture.

VII

And here we come to the existential tragedy of the subject, a tragedy linked to the principle of uncertainty, or rather *two* principles of uncertainty: the first principle of uncertainty is that the I is neither primary nor pure. The *computo* does not exist outside of all the physical, chemical, and biological operations which constitute the auto-eco-organization of the bacterium. The *computo* did not descend from on high upon the bacterium, and neither was it installed by an engineer. All dimensions of existence are inseparable. The *computo* is necessary to the existence of the bacterium which is necessary to the existence of the *computo*. In other words, the compute emerges from something that doesn't compute, just as life emerges from something that is not living, namely physico-chemical organization acquires distinctively living characteristics, and in so doing acquires the possibility of computing in the first person. This means that when "I" speak, it is also a "we" that speaks, the we of that warm collectivity of which we are a part. But there is not only the "we": "They" also speak when "I" speak, a "they" which is the voice of a more cold and anonymous collectivity. In every human "I" there is a "we" and a "they." The I, therefore, is not something pure, nor is it alone. The I could not speak were it not for "they."

And there is obviously the "it" which speaks too. "*Das Es*." What is the it? The it is a biological machine, something organizational that is even more anonymous than the "they." Thus, every time I speak, "they" speak and "it" speaks, which has led some to think that the "I" doesn't exist. Unidimensional thinking only sees the "they" and so is blind to the "I." Conversely, those who only see the "I" dissolve the "they" and the "it", whereas a complex understanding of the subject allows us to join together, in an indissoluble manner, the "I" with the "we", and both of these with the "they" and the "it." Such an understanding, however, involves the principle of uncertainty, since I am never completely sure to what extent it is I who am speaking, or if in fact I am being spoken by something which speaks for me, something stronger than me and which speaks at just that moment when I believe myself to be speaking. We can never be sure. To what extent is it I who speak? It is for this reason that we must reinterpret Freud's dictum to reveal its full meaning and fundamental inspiration: "Where It was, I have become." This does not mean that the It must disappear, or that the "they" must disappear. No, it means that the "I" is something which must *emerge*.

There is a second principle of uncertainty: it is that the subject oscillates between everything and nothing. It is everything for itself. By virtue of the principle of egocentricity, it is at the center of the world, and is the center of the world. Objectively, however, from the perspective of the Universe, it is nothing, or at best something minuscule and ephemeral. On the one hand, there is this unheard of privilege which the I accords to itself, and on the other, the consciousness that we can have that this most sacred and fundamental of things, our most precious treasure, is nothing at all. We stand divided between egoism and altruism, and at any moment we are capable of sacrificing this treasure for something which possesses a richer subjectivity, or even for something which transcends subjectivity and which we might call truth, or the belief in truth: The Faith! God! Socialism! Etc.

The condition of the individual-subject is clearly paradoxical. The death of each individual is, for it, equivalent to the death of the Universe. It is the total death of a universe. At the same time, this death reveals the fragility, the near nothingness of this entity that is the subject. By the same token, however, we are capable of seeking out this death when we offer our lives to the Nation, to Humanity, to God or to Truth.

Let me conclude by apologizing for having said at once too much and too little. I would add only that we must effect an overall and ongoing conceptual reconstruction if we are to grasp the notion of the subject. If we do not begin from biological organization, from the cognitive dimension, computation, the computo, the principle of exclusion, the principle of identity, etc., we will never succeed in grounding the notion of the subject in an empirical and logical manner. The organizational qualities of the subject demand that we associate antagonistic concepts: exclusion and inclusion, the I, the they, and the it. This requires what I have called *complex* thinking, which is to say a thinking that is capable of unifying concepts which repel one another and are otherwise catalogued and isolated in separate compartments. Now, we all know that compartmentalized and disciplinary thinking still dominates the world. This kind of thinking obeys a paradigm which rules according to the principles of disjunction, separation, and reduction. It is not possible, according to these principles, truly to grasp the subject. Nor is it possible to grasp the ambivalences, the uncertainties, or the inadequacies which pertain to the notion of the subject, or simultaneously to recognize its central and yet peripheral character, or the way it is both significant and insignificant. It is this kind of effort that is required, I believe, for the notion of the subject truly to emerge. Without such effort, we cannot but continue to split it apart, to transcendentalize it, and we will never come to understand it.

7

THE EPISTEMOLOGY
OF COMPLEXITY

Translated by Sean M. Kelly

I

When someone says, "It's complex. It's very complex!", the word "complex" does not constitute an explanation, but rather indicates the difficulty in explaining. The word serves to designate something we really can't explain, but that we shall call: "complex." For this reason, if there really is a complex form of thinking, it won't be a thinking capable of opening all doors (like those keys that open safes and cars). It will, on the contrary, be a thinking wherein difficulty is forever present. Deep down, of course, one would like to avoid complexity, and instead have simple ideas, simple laws and formulas to understand and explain what's going on around and within us. However, as such laws and formulas are increasingly inadequate, we are faced with the challenge of complexity, a challenge that demands, to begin with, a clarification of what "complexity" might mean. And here we already have a problem: Is there a single complexity? Or many complexities?

One could say that there is complexity wherever one finds a tangle of actions, interactions, and feedback. And this tangle is such that, even with the aid of a computer, it would be impossible to grasp all of the processes involved. But there is also another complexity that has to do with the existence of random phenomena (which cannot be rendered determinate and which add empirical uncertainty to thinking). One could say that there is an empirical pole and a logical pole, and that difficulty at either end (or both at once) signals the presence of complexity.

As to empirical difficulties, there is a wonderful example from meteorology, known as the "butterfly effect": the beating of a butterfly's wings in Australia can, through a series of causal chains and their effects, provoke a tornado in Buenos Aires, for example. At bottom, this kind of complexity was what Pascal clearly realized three centuries ago: "All things depend upon one another. All things are both mediated and immediate, as each thing is linked to everything else through a bond that connects even the most distantly separated. In such conditions I consider it as impossible to know the parts without a knowledge of the whole as it is to know the whole without a knowledge of the parts." This is the primary complexity; nothing is really isolated in the universe. Everything is interrelated. We shall find this complexity in the world of physics, but also in the world of politics since, as we shall see, we are now in the Planetary Era where what happens at any point on the Globe can have repercussions on every other point as well.

The logical problem appears as soon as deductive logic is unable to furnish a proof within a given thought-system and when insurmountable contradictions arise. Such is the case, for instance, in micro-physics. It was a historic moment when, at the turn of the century, two conceptions of elementary matter collided: waves versus particles. The critical moment arrived when Niels Bohr said that these two contradictory conceptions were in fact complementary since, empirically, the two phenomena (waves and particles) manifest under different conditions and must, despite their mutual incompatibility, be considered together. Here, then, are unavoidable complexities with which we must come to terms.

Here I would recall Pascal, summarizing him somewhat simplistically: "The whole is in everything, and vice versa." Which means: "Give up! For you will certainly end up totally confused!" And yet this phrase, "The whole is in everything and vice versa," can become intelligible, as long as we accept the following proposition: not only is the part in the whole, but the whole is also in the part. But how? Consider the following examples: every cell of the body is a part of the whole body as organism, yet each cell contains the totality of genetic information pertaining to the body as a whole, which means that the whole is also in the part. Each individual within a society is part of a whole, but societies, as wholes, depend upon the internalization of cultural norms, prohibitions, language, etc. Once again, the whole is in the part. From a cosmic standpoint, we human beings are a part of the cosmic totality: the particles that came into being during the first moments of the universe make up the atoms of our bodies. The carbon atoms required for life were formed within a sun that preceded our own. In other words, the totality of the history of the cosmos is within us, though we remain a lost and infinitesimal part of the cosmos. And yet, we are singular beings because the principle, "the whole is in the parts," does not mean that the part is a pure and simple reflection of the whole. Each part preserves its uniqueness and individuality as it contains, in a sense, the whole.

II

The complexity in question is evidently highly problematical, and particularly so given the prevailing historical and cultural context. We have learned at school how to separate areas of study: history, geography, physics, etc. Well and good! At the same time, however, a closer look tells us that, experimentally, chemistry coincides with micro-physics. We know that history always takes place on a given territory with its associated geography. And we now know that geography involves the history of the cosmos spelled out in countrysides, mountains, and planes. . . . Thus, we must indeed distinguish between various areas of study, but we must avoid absolute separations. We have learned well how to separate. We separate the object from its environment, as we isolate it from the observer who considers it. Ours is a disjunctive and reductive thinking: we seek to explain the whole by virtue of the parts of which it is constituted. We want to eliminate the problem of complexity. This makes for a profound obstacle, rooted as it is in a way of thinking imposed on us from childhood, developed at school and in the universities and enshrined through specialization; and thus our societies are increasingly governed by experts and specialists.

The problem here, and it is a grave one, is that specialists are excellent at resolving problems that arise within their specialties, but only on condition that they avoid interfering factors from neighboring specialties, and only as long as no new problem element presents itself. For as soon as there is anything new or interfering, the expert tends to fail somewhat more frequently than the non-expert. We have thus come to scorn general ideas since, it is claimed, such ideas are "built in the air," are empty and lacking any "proof." Experts, however, cannot do without general ideas; they have general ideas about life, the world, love, men, women, politics. . . . It is only that theirs are the poorest of general ideas since they are never put into question nor subject to control. One cannot live without general ideas, by which I mean ideas about human nature, about life, about society. For the last twenty or thirty years now, classical science has decomposed the cosmos, decomposed life, saying it doesn't exist, that there only molecules, genes. . . . Classical science has decomposed society; its fragmented demographic and economic studies have decomposed the global problem and even humanity itself which, if not nearly an illusion, could hardly merit the attention of the specialists. But we certainly cannot renounce the fundamental questions that human beings have always asked from the time we began to think, to gaze at the starry heavens, from the time that, as citizens, we asked ourselves how to build a better society, or at least a less evil one; from the time we asked: "But where do we come from? What is the meaning of life?"

We cannot live our lives dodging these questions as though they were stupid or uncalled for. They can, of course, be eliminated, but from then on the only function of knowledge becomes manipulation. Moreover, as Husserl clearly saw, as soon as science, or rather techno-science, stops putting itself into question, as soon as it ceases reflecting on its evolution, its foundations and wider implications, it becomes a blind machine. Paradoxically, this modern science, which has brought so much to light about the cosmos, about the stars, about bacteria, and so many other things, is completely blind to itself and its powers, and we know not whither it is leading us.

III

But if there are such forms of thinking which lead us ever to reduce, split, and obscure the great questions within us, it is because our thinking is ruled by a profound and hidden paradigm without our being aware of it. We believe we see what is real; but we see in reality only what this paradigm allows us to see, and we obscure what it requires us not to see. Today, in this century, we are faced with the following question: Are we witnessing the start of a paradigm shift, one tending in the direction of complexity? I believe we can approach this question from three different fronts—that of the natural sciences, that of the human sciences, and that of politics.

Why believe that a paradigm shift has begun in the natural sciences? Because, in this century, we have witnessed the collapse of what was the central dogma of classical physics. For Descartes and Newton, the physical world was perfect. Why? Because it was the expression of divine perfection. Even after Laplace had chased God from the world, he continued to believe the world was perfect, or rather he transferred this divine attribute to the world. For Laplace, the world was a perfectly deterministic machine whose every movement, whether past or future, could in principle be known with absolute certainty (with the help, that is, of an all-powerful demon). It was a totally ordered mechanism. Any disorder could only be illusory or merely apparent. This world was made up of little, indivisible, elementary blocks—that is, atoms. But we see how this world has collapsed, and from two sides at once! From the bottom, when we realized that the atom was not a block but an extremely complex system of particles, themselves highly complex entities, on the border between the material and the non-material, with this strange quality of appearing now as a wave, and now as a particle. And in the micro-physical world, what we see is a cloud of indeterminacies from which we can derive only a statistical orderliness.

At the level of the cosmos, a mechanical and eternal world collapsed thirty years ago with the discovery of the galaxies receding, with the discovery of the cosmic background radiation at 3 degrees Kelvin, with the hypothesis that this world was born in a primal fire, or from a small initial fluctuation in the Void, and that this world emerges from a mixture of order and disorder. It was born from disorder in the sense that it arose through combustion and with intense heat (which involves the disordered agitation of particles or atoms). But it is equally a question of order in that certain particles become associated when they meet within the surrounding disorder, and it is at this moment that a few major principles are constituted which allow for the formation of nuclei along with galaxies and stars.

Our universe is thus the fruit of what I have called a dialogic of order and disorder. Dialogic in the sense that it is a question of two completely heterogeneous, mutually exclusive, notions, granting an essential role to that which seemed obscene to the determinists. The latter protest: "How's this? Disorder? But there's no disorder. It's an illusion!" Well, disorder not only exists, it even plays a productive role in the universe. And this is the most amazing phenomenon. It is this dialogic of order and disorder that produces all of the living organizations in the universe. We now can see that what's true in the physical world is equally true for the origins of life which seems to have appeared in the midst of whirlpools, eruptions, and storms, some four billion years ago. We are thus compelled to work with disorder and uncertainty, and in so doing realize that this does not mean letting ourselves be overwhelmed by them; it means, rather, finally coming to terms with them by means of a more dynamic and complex form of thinking. Hegel said that true thinking is thinking that looks death straight in the face. We could add that true thinking is thinking that looks disorder and uncertainty straight in the face.

And in fact, we are now witnessing the birth of a new type of science which differs considerably from the classical variety. I would draw attention to three examples. The first is cosmology which demands the integration of data from observational astronomy, from radio telescopes, along with data from particle accelerators in micro-physics, with the goal of trying to imagine what conditions prevailed during, say, the formation of the first physical elements when the universe came into being. Cosmology is thus a reflective science constituted from diverse elements. The second example is furnished by the Earth sciences: geology, meteorology, vulcanology, and seismology were, as recently as thirty years ago, quite separate disciplines. That is, until the moment when, thanks to the theory of plate tectonics, we conceived of the Earth as a living system (not in the sense of biological organisms such as we are, but with a life of its own, with its regulations, its self-production, its transformations and its history), which allowed all of these disciplines to become interconnected around the idea of the Earth as a system. The science of ecology is equally new, since its central concept is that of the ecosystem. An ecosystem is the organizational ensemble that constitutes itself by means of interactions between living beings—unicellular organisms, plants, animals—and the geophysical conditions of a specific place, a biotope, an ecological niche. On a wider scale, ecosystems are themselves part of a vast system called the biosphere which has its own life and regulations.

In other words, here are sciences whose objects are systems. What this tells us is that we must generalize the notion of system so as to replace the closed, monotonous, and uniform idea of objects. All the objects we know are in fact systems, which means they possess a certain organization.

IV

At this point we have to deal with a problem that has long been ignored because it was thought that organization is a function of order pure and simple. In fact, organization is that which binds the system together, a system being any whole constituted by a grouping and linking of different elements.

And the idea that destroys any attempt at reductionistic explanation is that the whole has a number of properties and qualities that the parts do not have in isolation. A bacterium has qualities and properties of self-production, of movement, of feeling, and self-repair that the isolated macromolecules of which it is constituted in no way possess. We can call these qualities "emergents" since they only come into being with the whole. These emergent qualities can feed back on the parts. I have said that society is a whole whose qualities feed back on the individuals by means of language, culture, and education. The whole is therefore more than the sum of the parts. At the same time, however, the whole is less than the sum of the parts since the organization of the whole imposes constraints and inhibitions upon the parts that constitute it and which no longer possess their total freedom. A social organization imposes its laws, its taboos, and prohibitions on the individuals who cannot do everything they might desire to do. Thus, the whole is at once more and less than the sum of its parts. With this little word, "organization," we are presented with a conceptual complexity that enjoins us, in each case, to determine both the advantages and the constraints, and in this way to avoid glorifying the biggest organizations. In fact, if a very large organization imposes constraints that are too strict, it is preferable to look to the smaller organizations ("Small is beautiful!"), where one finds fewer constraints on the parts or the individuals. All of which leads us to consider the differences between organizations and to judge them on the basis of the freedom or the constraints that they involve.

At this point I would draw attention to the fundamental difference between living machines—which I have described in terms of self-eco-organization—and the artificial ones we fabricate in our factories. This difference was already pointed out by Von Neumann as early as the 1950s. von Neumann began with the following paradox: an artificial machine is made of extremely dependable components, all of which have been fabricated and tested. We choose the most resistant, the most solid, and those best adapted to the work for which they are designed. Artificial machines begin to deteriorate as soon as they begin to function. By contrast, a living machine, such as a bacterium, is made of barely dependable components. Its molecules deteriorate very easily. Whereas artificial machines begin to deteriorate as soon as they begin to function, a living machine, from the very beginning, undergoes a certain development. It too will finally deteriorate, but its wear and tear will be of a different kind. Why is this? The answer was given by Heraclitus over 2,000 years ago in this extremely dense formula: "Life from death, death from life." As I see it, "Life from death" means that, although its molecules deteriorate, a living organism is capable of producing new molecules that rejuvenate it. We are constantly being rejuvenated. Every heart-beat irrigates the entire organism with blood that has been detoxified by the lungs. In other words, we are rejuvenated sixty times a minute, and several times a year our molecules are rejuvenated. We live off the death of the cells that rejuvenate us. But why, then, do we die? Because all of this rejuvenation is, in the long run, very tiring. This is why, unhappily, we die. We die from living.

Von Foerster drew attention to another characteristic of living machines. It is a matter of non-trivial machines. "A trivial machine," he said, "is a machine whose outputs can be known from its inputs. Even without knowing what's going on inside the machine, you can predict its behavior." We are all familiar with the behavior of trivial machines. Living machines often behave like trivial machines. Our behavior is predictable: we go to work in the morning, more or less on time, in a quite foreseeable manner.

But sometimes we do things that are completely unexpected. I remember a very good friend of mine about to be married by the mayor of Paris, who asked the bride, "Do you wish to marry Mr. So and So?" "I do," she replied. Then to the groom, "Do you wish to marry Miss So and So?" He hesitated. He has a daisy in his hand, plucking its petals one by one, saying, "yes, no, yes, no . . . " and ending with "no," he says, "I'm sorry." An admittedly rare occurrence.

But then again, there are many historical moments and all of them are the result of the non-trivial workings of the human machine. When someone says that one should not punish an offense, but rather turn the other cheek—that is, forgive—this is a non-trivial reaction that runs counter to the logic of vendetta, vengeance, and punishment.

Such, then, are the enormous differences between artificial and living machines. Artificial machines cannot tolerate disorder. As soon as one element becomes disordered, the machine comes to a halt. Living machines, by contrast, can tolerate a great quantity of disorder. For example, a ceaseless and uncontrolled proliferation of cells takes place within our bodies, but they do not (most of the time) develop into a cancer, because, at a certain moment, immunological defenses intervene and force them to stop reproducing. Human societies tolerate an enormous amount of disorder, and one aspect of this disorder is what we call freedom. We can thus make use of disorder as a necessary element in innovative and creative processes, because all innovation and creation must inevitably be seen as deviation and error from the perspective of a previously fixed system. Such, then, is the manner in which one must conceive of the fundamental complexity of all living reality.

I would add that, if one must consider not objects, but systems, this means that the system itself can be considered as a part of a polysystem or as contained within a specific environment or ecosystem. I have already said that our environment is inscribed within us. Here we must invoke the holographic principle: not only is the part within the whole, but the whole is in the part.

This principle, moreover, raises another essential point. Formerly, it was thought that, because we had eliminated the observer as a merely contingent element, we possessed a certain objective knowledge. However, we know that we only perceive reality—or what we perceive and call reality—thanks to the mental structures and patterns that allow us to organize our experience in temporal and spatial terms. We have acted as though the external world exists in itself and that our knowledge of it amounts to an accurate photographic image. But this way of thinking becomes completely untenable as soon as we realize that all knowledge is translation and reconstruction. All knowledge is translation in the sense that the stimuli which effect the eye are taken up by millions of distinct cells which together compose a message that is transmitted to the brain through the optic nerve using a binary code. All of these messages are received in different regions of the brain, are mixed and transformed to produce a perception or representation. Thus, there has been translation and reconstruction.

V

Here we enter the debate around constructivism. Personally, I am a co-constructivist, which means that I think we construct our perception of the world, but with the help of the world itself which, as it were, lends us a hand. This does not mean, however, that we can evade the status of knowledge as "translation" and "construction." It is amazing that our brain is completely enclosed within the cranium, that it does not communicate directly with the outside world, and this world sends stimuli which are transformed into messages, themselves transformed into information which in turn is transformed into perceptions. All of this is extremely important and holds for all knowledge. What's more, while developments within science seemed to indicate that the observer was to be forever banished, it was science itself that reintroduced it. It is Heisenberg's Uncertainty Principle which proves—and this, if I can put it this way, for purely physical reasons—that if we wish to make an observation at the micro-physical level, one must use photons which will disturb the particles being observed. In other words, there is a limit beyond which the observer becomes an interfering factor.

But more significantly, Niels Bohr and the representatives of the so-called Copenhagen Interpretation of Quantum Mechanics thought that what we know is not the world" itself, but the world along with our knowledge of it. We cannot isolate the world from our structures of knowing. Mind and world are inseparable. And this is particularly true of the human world. Sociology and anthropology can no longer claim to be "scientific" by the mere fact of analyzing questionnaires. It is evident that the observer must analyze itself while observing others. Take the case of anthropology. If anthropology was so aberrant at the beginning of this century, it was because anthropologists were persuaded that they were the masters of knowledge and rationality and, from their Western perspective, they found what they took to be an archaic world of grown children who lived in a purely animistic, "mystical," or neurotic manner. Levi-Bruhl said that those he called "primitives" in his publications lived in a state of "participation mystique." He never asked himself, as did Wittgenstein upon reading the works of James Frazer: "But how can it be that these savages who spend their time dancing, singing, performing ritual enchantments, and magical acts know equally well how to hunt with real arrows, with a true strategy and a true knowledge of the external world?" We did not realize that magic and rationality coexisted in these societies. We did not see, similarly, that there is magic as well as rationality in our society, and even within our rationality. Anthropologists must therefore situate themselves in the world they inhabit in order to try to understand the wholly strange world they will study.

But are things easier for sociologists who study their own society? Not in the least! Because sociologists are themselves part of a whole; they have a partial point of view. While they too in one sense include the whole, they are possessed by their own society. It is therefore necessary to exert an extraordinary mental effort to find a meta-point of view. But how to find a meta-point of view from within a given society? Obviously by knowing something about other societies: by studying past societies, by imagining possible or future societies, and contrasting them with the present one in order to decenter ourselves. And the point of view of complexity tells us precisely that it is crazy to believe we can know things from an omniscient point of view, from some supreme throne looking down upon the universe. There is no omniscient vantage point. But what we can do to avoid total relativism or ethnocentrism is to construct a meta-point of view. It is as though we were imprisoned in camps but still capable of building look-out towers and, from this perspective, could see the camp along with what's going on in the outside world. We can establish meta-points of view, however limited and fragile.

Sociological, anthropological, or any other form of knowledge must therefore attain to the meta-point of view. Here we have an absolute requirement which allows us to distinguish between a more simple mode of thinking—where one believes one possesses the truth, where one thinks that knowledge merely reflects what is, and where one has no need to know oneself to know the object—and complex knowing which demands a self-observing (and, I would add, self-criticizing) turn on the part of the observer-conceiver. Such, then, are some of the attainments and modifications necessary for a complex thinking.

VI

To return to the human problem: when one speaks of the human being, one has the sense of something generic and abstract. Human beings are, in the first place, somewhat bizarre, at once biological and non-biological beings. As a matter of convenience, we study the biological side of human beings in departments of biology and the cultural and psychological side in departments of humanities and psychology. Human beings have brains, which are biological organs, and minds, which are psychical ones. But these organs never meet, and people who study the brain do not realize they do so with the mind (and vice versa). This disjunction with which we live mutilates our vision. Moreover, the human being is not merely bio-cultural in nature. The relation between the species, society, and the individual is multidimensional. And this human being which our manuals have named "homo sapiens" is also "homo demens." As Castoriadis puts it: "A human being is that insane animal whose insanity has invented reason." The fact is that one cannot draw a firm boundary between wisdom and folly. What, for instance, constitutes a wise life? Clearly no one has provided a universally satisfactory answer to this question.

And in these human beings, who are at once wise and demented, there are two kinds of thinking inextricably mixed: a thinking which I shall call rational, empirical, and technical, that has existed from prehistory and precedes humanity (since animal behavior makes use of observation, reasoning, and techniques) but which, evidently, humans in particular have particularly developed. We have, as well, a symbolic, mythological, and magical kind of thinking. Both kinds of thinking are always to some degree co-active. Anyone interested in the human psyche knows that dreams, fantasies, and delusions are an essential part of human nature. They are not mere smoke and vapor, but are woven into the very fabric of life. "We are of such stuff as dreams are made on," as Shakespeare says. Why forget this? Why do we remain so close-minded? Why do we continue to see human beings solely in terms of their social or professional status, their standard of living, their age, gender, or however else they figure in opinion polls? Every human being, even the most anonymous, is a veritable cosmos. Not only because the swarm of interactions in her brain is larger than all the interactions among stellar bodies in the cosmos, but also because she harbors within herself a fabulous and unknown world.

For quite some time, the superiority of literature over the human sciences lay in its recognition of this truth, and this at a time when the human and social sciences had completely annihilated the existence of the individual. Today, however, biology is revealing to us the extraordinary anatomical and psychological diversity of individuals. In a lovely text, "Lessons for Primitive People," Niels studied an Amazonian tribe which had lived isolated for five hundred years. He found individuals as different from one another as those in a Paris metro or the streets of Buenos Aires.

The singular, the concrete, the passions and suffering of the flesh are the life-blood of the novel. When Balzac tried to understand people by analyzing their faces, along with their styles of behavior, their furniture and their surroundings, he was clearly doing something complex. When Stendhal showed the importance of small, apparently insignificant details which nevertheless play such an important role in life, he was working with complexity. When Tolstoy showed individual destinies overlapping with the sweep of world history, as in the case of Prince Andre in *War and Peace*, he succeeded in linking the individual soul with the historical destiny of the world. And Dostoievsky, in revealing the irregularities, the sudden movements from one part of ourselves to another, shows how impossible it is to rationalize a human being down to a formula. The great novelists have shown the way of complexity, and even if they haven't done so conceptually or in a philosophical or scientific manner, they have contributed something essential to philosophical and scientific thinking.

VII

I would like to turn now to the problem of political complexity. To begin with, politics has traditionally been seen as the art of governing, and there was a time, especially during the French Revolution, when it became something more than the art of governing. For politics can give something important to citizens. It can give them liberty, equality, and fraternity, something which improves society. At the same time, Saint Just has remarked that, "All the arts have produced their marvels, but the art of governing is alone in having produced only monsters." Since the French Revolution, however, many human factors have entered politics which formerly were left out of consideration. Such is the case with demographics. Ought one, for instance, to legislate against a declining birth rate? Should one encourage abortions? Is it necessary to control birth rates? The demographic problem, which had been a biological problem, has entered into politics. The ecological problem, which at one point seemed a purely external problem, has become a political one from the moment we understood that the degradations we are imposing on the biosphere have social and political consequences, whether it be the question of the local pollution of a river or lake that poses a concrete problem for a city, a region, or whether it be the global problems of the biosphere.

An even greater invasion of the political sphere has begun. That it is now possible to make a test-tube baby, or take the sperm from an unknown or deceased person to make a baby, raises fundamental questions which unsettle what was once most stable in our lives. Formerly, one knew what a father was, and what a mother. But today. . . . Recently, in one case among many, I heard of a woman becoming a mother and grandmother at once, because she had borne her daughter's embryo. And there are other similarly distressing cases which become political problems. All of the sciences, as they develop, create political problems. It is obvious that the development of nuclear physics produced the political problems of nuclear energy, problems of life and death and of thermo-nuclear weapons. There is, moreover, the fact that our nations are tending to become welfare states, taking more control of the lives of individuals, and correcting for natural disasters by compensating victims of bad crops or floods. Politics is thus extensively involved in the field of social protection.

Practically, what this means is that politics has become terribly complex. It is now concerned with all dimensions of humanity. And what happens in such a situation? There is either the rise of totalitarian politics which imposes the dominance of a single party ideology or, as tends to be the case in our society, politics becomes increasingly technocratic and econocratic. In any case, we see that, under current conditions of international economic competition, problems which had formerly been political in nature, though secondarily so, have become major concerns: the stability of national currencies, the balancing of imports and exports. Politics is overwhelmed by economic concerns and this makes economic and technical thinking predominant. It is thus absolutely necessary to develop a complex form of thinking capable of understanding that politics has become multidimensional.

And this is occurring as we enter ever deeper into the Planetary Era, which is to say into the innumerable interconnections among all the fragments of the planet. There is solidarity in conflict. For what has produced the Planetary Era? The two World Wars. And we can see here as well not only the part in the whole, but also the whole in the part. In France, for example, I get up in the morning and have a coffee from Brazil or Ethiopia, or tea from India, turn on my Japanese radio and listen to news from around the world, put on my cotton shirt that was made in Hong Kong, and thus throughout the whole day, without knowing it, I am a citizen of the Earth. But you might say to me: "What about all these poor people who live in shantytowns? Are they citizens of the Earth?" Well, yes. Theirs is a planetary existence of the most horrible kind. It is the development of industrial growth which has developed the uprooting of rural life. It is the quest for profit which has provoked the disappearance of small proprietors and their rush to the shantytowns: cayampas, favelas, etc. And all of this means that these people, in their destitution, are living the planetary tragedy. How can we, therefore, strive for an exclusively national politics, without thinking about the continental environment? How is possible today to conceive of an economic and ecological politics without it being from a metanational point of view? Contemporary politics is confronted with this planetary complexity.

Finally, I would add that politics has lost what once gave it a false certainty. It has lost the sense of a guaranteed future. In fact, one must recognize that it was not only the totalitarian system of the USSR which promised a glorious future (a future which, as we all know, collapsed). Our Western societies lived by the idea, not of the laws of history in the simplistic manner of dogmatic Marxism, but by the idea of inevitable, necessary, and guaranteed progress. We thought that there could be a few zigzags, a few stops, but that the future was guaranteed. Why? Well, because science was developing, and all that it could develop was rationality and benefits. Because democracy could only go on developing. But today, after Hiroshima, after genetic engineering, we are becoming aware that science is ambivalent, that it can just as easily destroy humanity as help it. We know that rationality does not grow as a matter of course. It can regress, can take on insane forms of rationalization, which is to say the form of a closed logical system, incapable of seeing reality. It is a question here of the great crisis and loss of the future. Why do we see religious fundamentalisms mixed up with awakening nationalisms? Because when one has lost the future, one latches onto the past. We are thus in an era when all the old formulas, such as "The future belongs to us," or "we must do such and such," have fallen to pieces and where politics is wedded to complexity. Politics, in fact, has lost its sovereignty: it is necessary to speak of the ecology of politics.

Politics will henceforth find itself afloat on a sea of interactions, and upon which it will have to learn to navigate.

VIII

This brings us to a fundamental principle of complexity—namely, the ecology of action. This principle tells us that action escapes the will of the actor to enter into the play of inter-retro-actions within society at large. In the France of 1789, for example, the aristocracy sought to profit from the weakening of royal power and provoked the convening of the Estates General representing three orders: the Nobility, the Clergy, and the Third Estate. Up to that point, the clergy and nobility had held the majority, but once the three orders were convened, the Third Estate, which was the most populous of the three, decided that the vote would go by head count and not by order. A National Assembly was constituted and the aristocratic initiative was transformed into its opposite: a democratic revolution. More recently, we have witnessed how the putsch of August 1991 in Moscow triggered events running counter to those intended, which is to say the liquidation of the power of the communist party and of the KGB. In this way action escapes the will of the actor.

There are two corollaries that flow from this principle. The first is that the level of maximum efficacy of the action is always at the beginning of its development. This is why, if one wishes to enact reforms, one must do so quickly. The second corollary is that the ultimate consequences of an action are not foreseeable. It is, therefore, under such conditions that one can grasp the epistemological reversal I have in mind. Politics does not rule. It must navigate by sight, which is what is evoked, etymologically, in the word "cybernetic." But this doesn't only mean that politics must navigate day by day; it must have an idea that lights the way like a beacon. It cannot make programs for the future since such programs are abstract and mechanistic projections that are thwarted by actual events. Nevertheless, we must project values, motivating ideas and ideas of power.

Actions, moreover, always involve a strategy. And here we must distinguish clearly between a program and a strategy. In so doing, we once again light upon that which sets apart simplifying from complex thinking. A program establishes a series of actions which are decided a priori and which must begin to function one after the other without variation. Obviously, a program functions quite well when environmental conditions remain constant and especially in the absence of perturbations. A strategy, by contrast, is an action scenario which can be modified in the light of new information or chance events as they arise. In other words, strategy is the art of working with uncertainty. In terms of thinking, strategy is the art of thinking with and in uncertainty. The strategy of action is the art of acting in uncertainty. To be sure, there is a difference between thinking and acting, as there are many modes of action which are complex in fact, though not in theory.

As an illustration, I would mention a popular game that I have come to appreciate, namely, soccer. The strategy of a soccer team does not consist in a program to make goals, since it is obvious that the other team has the same intentions. It does not consist in constructing a game, but in playing a game that will deconstruct the adversary's moves while the latter seeks to deconstruct the game that you are playing. In this situation, an important role will be played by the errors of the adversary. In the same way that a good judo player uses the enemy's energy to throw him, the good soccer player will use every weakness and error on the part of the adversary in order to make a goal. In other words, the soccer matches that so many people watch every week demonstrate something of the nature of complexity.

Our vision and our perception are very complex processes. While looking at something in front of us, we are capable of fixing our gaze on a single element, then of taking in the whole thing, to sweep outwards and see the relation between one thing and another. We are capable seeing with our eyes in a complex manner. However, we seem incapable of thinking in a complex manner. It is in this direction, I believe—the direction of a thinking which thinks itself—that we must tend if we are to make any progress on the path of complexity.

IX

I will conclude by saying that complex thinking is not omniscient thinking. It is, on the contrary, a thinking which knows it is always local, situated in a given time and place. Neither is it a complete thinking, for it knows in advance that there is always uncertainty. By the same token, it avoids the arrogant dogmatism which rules non-complex forms of thinking. Complex thinking, however, does not lead to a resigned skepticism, since, by completely breaking with the dogmatism of certainty, it throws itself courageously into the adventure of uncertain thinking and participates in the uncertain adventure upon which, from its birth, humanity has been embarked. We must learn to live with uncertainty rather than do what we have been taught to do for millennia and seek, through whatever means, to avoid it. Of course, it is a good thing to have certainty, but if it is a false certainty, then this is very bad. Thus, the real task is to favor strategies over programs.

We are, perhaps, living through a great paradigm shift. Perhaps. It is difficult to determine with any certainty, since a great revolution in the principles of thinking takes a long time. It is, or will be, a very slow, multiple, and difficult revolution. It has perhaps already begun, somewhat like that battle of Midway during the Second World War. This was a fascinating battle because the Japanese and American fleets fought each other over hundreds of miles, but the ships were greatly separated from one another. Japanese planes attacked American boats and American planes attacked Japanese boats, with Japanese submarines against American submarines. . . . It was a situation of each against all, a struggle that baffles description and one whose global physiognomy eluded the perception of the admirals. At a certain moment, the Japanese admiral said, "I have had many losses. It is best to beat a retreat." So, seeing the Japanese fleet beginning to retreat, the American admiral said, "We've won!" And here we are in another battle of Midway, a battle which is not yet won. We are witnessing a great struggle between, on the one hand, ancient and withered ways of thinking (and you know how strong such ways of thinking are, how, in their sclerosis, they offer so much resistance), and on the other hand, new, embryonic forms of thinking (which, in their newness, are terribly fragile and in danger of dying). We stand on the threshold of a new beginning. We are not in the last stages of the history of thinking, nor have we reached the limits of the human spirit. We are, rather, still in its prehistory. We are not in the final struggle. We are, rather, still in the initial engagement. We are in an initial period where it is necessary to recalibrate our perspectives on knowledge and politics in a manner that is worthy of humanity in the Planetary Era, so that we can come to be as humanity. And here, as I have said, we must learn to work with chance and uncertainty.

I will conclude with two metaphors: the first comes from Jules Michelet who, in a lovely book about the sea, imagines two whales mating. He had never seen two whales mating, and so he thought that, for the impregnation to occur, it would be necessary for the couple simultaneously to assume a vertical position. Obviously, there would be many unsuccessful attempts, and the whales would have to start over repeatedly before achieving impregnation. In reality, the situation is much more prosaic—the whales mate in a horizontal position. What this metaphor suggests, however, is that the world of political action does not possess the physical efficiency of a hammer driving a nail. We are, rather, like the poor whales struggling to keep the right position. And we should rejoice when we get it right.

The second metaphor is that of the chrysalis. For a caterpillar to become a butterfly, it must enclose itself within a chrysalis. But what goes on inside the caterpillar is fascinating: the immune system of the caterpillar starts to destroy everything that had been caterpillar, including the digestive system, since the butterfly will not eat the same food as the caterpillar. The only thing left is the nervous system. Thus, the caterpillar destroys itself as caterpillar in order to construct itself as butterfly. And once the butterfly, still half paralyzed, succeeds in breaking open the chrysalis, you see it there, its glistening wings all stuck together. You wonder whether or not it will make it. And just when you had given up hope of ever seeing it flutter its wings, it suddenly takes flight.

APPENDIX 1

THE CONCEPT OF SYSTEM

Translated by Sean M. Kelly

Objects give way to systems. Instead of essences and substances, organization; instead of simple and elementary units, complex unities; instead of aggregates forming bodies, systems of systems of systems. The object is no longer a form-essence or a matter-substance. There is no longer a form-mould that sculpts the identity of the object from the outside. The idea of form is preserved, yet transformed; form is the totality of organized complex unity that manifests itself phenomenally as whole in time and space; Gestalts form among elements of internal organization, of the conditions, pressures, and constraints of the environment. Form is no longer conceived in terms of essence but in terms of existence and organization. Likewise, materiality is no longer reducible to the idea of substance enclosed within form. However, materiality has not vanished; it has enriched itself in its dereification. All systems are constituted by physical elements and processes. The idea of organized matter only becomes fully intelligible within the more complex idea of self-organizing *physis*.

Thus the Aristotelian model (form/substance) and the Cartesian model (simplifiable and decomposable objects)—both subjacent to our conception of objects—do not provide the system's principles of intelligibility. The system cannot be grasped as pure unity of intelligibility. The system cannot be grasped as pure unity nor as absolute identity, nor as decomposable composite. We need a systemic concept that expresses at once unity, multiplicity, totality, diversity, organization, and complexity.

1. BEYOND HOLISM AND REDUCTIONISM: THE RELATIONAL CIRCUIT

We have already said and it bears repeating: Neither the description nor the explanation of a system can take place at the level of parts, conceived as isolated entities, linked merely by actions and reactions. Because the compositional rules of the system are not additive but transformative, analytic de-composition into elements decomposes the system in the process.

Also, the reductionistic explanation of a complex whole in terms of its simple elements disarticulates, disorganizes, simplifies, and, in the final analysis, destroys what makes up the reality of the system itself: articulation, organization, complex unity. It ignores the transformations effected on the parts; it ignores the whole as whole, emergent qualities (which are conceived as the simple effects of combined actions), as well as latent or virulent antagonisms. Atlan's remark concerning living organisms applies to all systems: "The simple fact of analyzing an organism according to its constituent elements entails a loss of information about that organism" (Atlan, 1972, p. 262).

It is not a question of underestimating the resounding successes of the reductionistic perspective; the search for the basic element led to the discovery of the molecule, then the atom, then the particle, etc. The search for manipulable units and verifiable effects permitted, in fact, the manipulation of all systems through manipulation of their elements. In the process, however a shadow was cast over organization, and obscurity was cast over complexity. In the end, the elucidations of reductionistic science were paved by obscurantism. Systems theory reacted to reductionism with its idea of the whole, but believing it had surpassed reductionism, its "holism" merely brought about a reduction to the whole, from which arose not only its blindness to the parts as parts but its myopia with respect to organization as organization, and its ignorance of the complexity at the heart of any global unity.

In either case, reductionistic or holist explanation seeks to simplify the problem of complex unity. The one reduces explanation of the whole to the properties of the parts conceived in isolation. The other reduces the properties of the parts to the properties of the whole, also conceived in isolation. These two mutually repelling explanations each arose out of the same paradigm.

The conception that is revealed here places us at once beyond reductionism and holism, and summons a principle of intelligibility that integrates the portion of truth included in each; there should neither be annihilation of the whole by the parts nor of the parts by the whole. It is essential, therefore, to clarify the relations between parts and whole, where each term refers back to the other: "I consider it as impossible," said Pascal, "to know the parts without knowing the whole, as to know the whole without a precise knowledge of the parts." In the twentieth century, reductionist and holist ideas still do not measure up to the level of such a formulation.

The truth of the matter is that, even more than mutually referring to one another, the interrelation that links explanation of the parts to that of the whole, and vice versa, is an invitation to recursive description and explanation; that is, description (explanation) of the parts depends upon that of the whole, which depends upon that of the parts, and it is in the circuit that the description of explanation constitutes itself.

This signifies that neither one of the two terms is reducible to the other. Thus, if the parts must be conceived in function of the whole, they must also be conceived in isolation: a part has its proper irreducibility in relation to the system. It is necessary, moreover, to know the qualities or properties of the parts that are inhibited, virtualized, and, therefore, invisible at the heart of the system, not only to correctly understand the parts, but also to better understand the constraints, inhibitions, and transformations effected by the organization of the whole.

It is equally essential to move beyond the purely globalizing and enveloping idea of the whole. The whole is not just emergence. It has, as we shall see, a complex face, and here the idea of a macroscope (de Rosnay, 1975), or a conceptual point of view, which allows us to perceive, recognize, and describe global forms, becomes indispensable.

The explanatory circuit of whole/parts cannot, as we have just seen, do away with the idea of organization. It must, therefore, be enriched as follows:

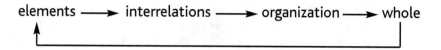

Elements must be defined at once according to their original characteristics, the interrelations in which they participate, the perspective of the organization in which they operate, and the perspective of the whole in which they are integrated. Conversely, organization must define itself in relation to the elements, the interrelations, the whole, and so forth. The circuit is *polyrelational*. In this circuit, organization plays a nuclearizing role with which we shall have to come to terms.

2. THE WHOLE IS NOT ALL

Scissions in the Whole (the Immersed and the Emergent, the Repressed and the Expressed).

Although emergents blossom as the phenomenal qualities of systems, organizational constraints immerse in a world of silence the characteristics that are inhibited, repressed, and compressed at the level of the parts. Thus all systems comprise an immersed, hidden, and obscure zone, teeming with stifled potentialities. The duality between the immersed and the emergent, the potential and the actual, the repressed and the expressed, is the source, in the great living and social polysystems, of scissions and dissociations between the sphere of the parts and that of the whole. The Freudian idea of the psychic unconscious, and the Marxist idea of the social unconscious, each reveal the bottomless pit hitherto concealed in the notions of identity and totality. The problem of the unconscious has its source—though only its source, for, as we shall see, it is not a question here of reducing everything to systemic terms—in this profound scission between the parts and the whole, between the world of the internal and that of the external.

In our own fashion, we recognize this duality when we distinguish between structure and form within a system. Our traditional logic, for its part, tends to reduce phenomenal characteristics, conceived as simple effects, to structural characteristics.

It is thus perfectly understandable that in considering social or biological systems in light of the relation infra/superstructure, one of the terms tends to be ignored or forgotten. Such ignorance can only be overcome through a recognition of the indissoluble solidarity that exists between both terms. We must, therefore, seek to understand the biological and sociological complexity of systems which, while remaining fundamentally unitary, comprise several levels of organization and existence through which such systems become equally multiple, dissociated, and, at the limit, inwardly antagonistic.

The Insufficient Whole

There are black holes in every totality—blind spots, zones of shadow, and ruptures. Totalities harbor internal divisions that are not merely the divisions between its distinguishable parts. There are scissions that are potential sources of conflict and separation. It is extremely difficult to grasp the idea of totality in a world dominated by reductionistic simplification. And once grasped, it would be ridiculous to conceive of it in a simplified and euphoric manner. The true totality is always fissured and incomplete. The true conception of totality recognizes the insufficiency of the totality. This is the great advance of Adorno over Hegel: "The totality is the non-truth."

The Uncertain Whole

Finally—and I shall return to this idea from another angle—the whole is uncertain. It is uncertain because we can isolate only with great difficulty, and can never truly close off, a system from the systems of systems of systems to which it is linked and where it may appear at once as Koestler has done well to indicate, as whole and part of a larger whole. It is uncertain for systems of high biological complexity with regard to the relation of individual/species, and especially for homo sapiens—that trisystemic monster—which involves the interrelations and interactions between species, individual, and society. Where, in this case, is the whole? The answer cannot but be ambiguous, multiple, and uncertain. One can assuredly look upon society as whole and the individual as part. But one can also conceive of the individual as the central system and society as its ecosystem, its organizer-placenta, and this even more so as consciousness emerges at the level of the individual and not the social whole. Likewise, we can invert the hierarchy species/individual as concrete whole, the species being nothing more than a mechanical cycle for the reproduction of individuals. The matter is not easily settled. In fact, one must, not only out of prudence but also out of the sense of complexity, understand that these terms finalize one another, refer back to one another in a circuit that itself is the "true" system:

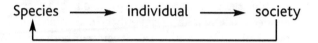

But such a system is a multiple totality, a polytotality, the three inseparable terms which are at the same time concurrent and antagonistic.

It follows that at certain moments, from certain angles and in certain cases, the part can be richer than the totality. Although a simplifying holism favors all totalities over its elements, we know that, henceforth, we need not necessarily favor all totalities over the components. We should consider the cost of the constraints on global emergents, and we should ask ourselves if these constraints do not annihilate the possibility of even richer emergents at the level of components. "The most profitable control system for the parts should not exclude the bankruptcy of the whole" (Beer, 1960, p. 16). The bankruptcy of imperial mega-systems might allow for the constitution of polycentric federal systems.

Finally, we need not favor the totality of totalities. What is the cosmos if not a totality in polycentric dispersion, the riches of which are disseminated into small archipelagos? It well seems that "small parts of the universe have a reflexive capacity larger than the whole" (Guenther, 1962, p. 383). It even seems, as Spencer Brown has suggested, that the capacity to reflect could only come about in a small, semi-detached part of the whole, thanks to the virtue and the vice of its remoteness, its distance, its open finitude with respect to the totality (Spencer-Brown, 1969). Consequently, it is again evident that the point of view of the totality by itself is partial and mutilating. Not only is the whole the "non-truth"—the truth of the whole is an actual as concrete individuality. The idea of totality becomes all the more beautiful and rich the more it ceases being totalitarian, the more it becomes incapable of being self-enclosed, the more it becomes complex. It is more radiant in the polycentrism of relatively autonomous parts than in the globalism of the whole.

3. BEYOND FORMALISM AND REALISM: FROM PHYSIS TO UNDERSTANDING, FROM UNDERSTANDING TO PHYSIS— THE SUBJECT SYSTEM AND THE OBJECT SYSTEM

The notion of system is subject to a double pressure. On the one hand, a smug realism considers the notion of system to be a reflection of the real characteristics of an empirical object, while on the other, formalism looks upon the system as an ideal model to be applied heuristically to phenomena without pre-judging their reality.

The reader is faced here with a fundamental problem associated with all phenomena and physical objects perceived and conceived by the human mind. In a sense, all descriptions upon which diverse observers agree refer to an objective reality. However, by the same token, the common description is related to the mental and logical categories and the perceptual structures without which there would be no description. This problem—the problem of the knowing of knowing—is treated at length in Volume III of *La Methode*. Nevertheless, we can already insert the notion of system, not within the alternative realism/formalism, but in a perspective where both terms are related to one another in a manner that is at once complementary, concurrent, and antagonistic.

The Rootedness in Physis

All systems, including those we isolate abstractly and arbitrarily from the sets of which they form a part (like the atom, which is otherwise a partially ideal object, or like the molecule) are necessarily rooted in physis.

Conditions of formation and existence are physical: gravitational and electromagnetic interactions, topological properties of forms, ecological conjunctures, energetic immobilizations and/or mobilizations. "A system cannot but be energetic," as Lupasco says; which is another way of saying: *a system is necessarily physical*. An ideal system, such as the one I am in the process of elaborating, pays its tribute in energy, provokes electrochemical modifications in my brain, corresponds to the stabilizing and morphogenetic properties of neural networks, and so on.

Finally, the insertion of the notion of emergence at the very heart of the theory of the system implies a rootedness in what is non-reducible and non-deducible, in what, in physical perception, resists our understanding and our rationalization. That is to say, it makes a rootedness in that aspect of the real that finds itself at the antipodes of the ideal.

There is, therefore, in the theory of the system that I am outlining something that is irreducibly linked at all levels to physical phenomenality: from below (originary interactions and the interrelations that maintain the system), from the periphery (the physical thresholds of existence beyond which the system disintegrates and transforms itself), and from above (emergents).

The System Is a Mental Abstraction

Just as all systems escape, from one angle or another, the mind of the observer to reveal their rootedness in physis, so all systems, even those two that seem phenomenally most evident—such as machines or organisms—reveal the activity of the mind insofar as the isolation of the system along with its concept are the result of abstractions effected by the mind of the observer/conceptualizer.

Ashby has remarked that "objects can display an infinity of systems of equal plausibility, distinct from one another according to their properties." (Ashby, 1956, p. 274) When I ask, "What am I?" I can conceive of myself as a physical system consisting of billions upon billions of atoms; a biological system of some thirty billion cells; an organismic system of certain organs; an element of my familial system, of my urban, professional, social, national, or ethnic system etc.

To be sure, certain distinctions have been established that permit the categorization of systems. Thus, one uses the terms:

- system, for anything that manifests autonomy and emergence with respect to that which is external to it
- sub-system, for any system that manifests subordination toward a system within which it is integrated as a part.
- supra-system, for any system that controls other systems, without integrating them within itself
- eco-system, for the systemic set whose interrelations constitute the environment within which the system is encompassed
- meta-system, for the system that results from the mutually transformative and encompassing interrelations between two previously independent systems.

In fact, however, the borders between these terms are not clearly defined. The terms themselves are interchangeable according to the framing, cutting, or point of view adopted by the observer of the system under consideration. The determination of systemic characteristics (sub-, eco-, etc.) depends upon selections, interests, choices, and decisions, which themselves depend upon the set of conditions that constitute the specific cultural and social context of the observer/conceptualizer.

There are cases where uncertainty pervades all characterization: is society the ecosystem of the individual, or is the latter the perishable and renewable constituent of the social system? Is the human species the super-system or the system? We cannot escape uncertainty but we can think and conceive of the concept *homo* as a triadic polysystem whose terms:

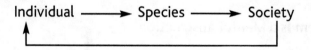

are at once complementary, concurrent, and antagonistic. This requires a theoretical construct and a complex conception of system that recognizes the active participation of the observer/conceptualizer.

There is always, therefore, something uncertain or arbitrary in the extraction, isolation, and definition of a system: there is always decision and choice, which introduces the category of the subject into the concept of system.

The system requires a subject to isolate it from the polysystemic swirl, to cut it out, to qualify and hierarchize it. It is doubly determined by, on one hand, a physical reality that cannot be reduced to the human mind, and on the other, by the very structures of this mind, by selective interests of the observer/subject along with the cultural and social context of the scientific consciousness.

The concept of system requires the full employment of the personal qualities of the subject in its communication with the object. It differs radically from the classical concept of the object, which referred uniquely either to the "real" or to ideal. Systems are profoundly related to the real. They are more real because they are more rooted in and linked with *physis* than the old quasi-artificial object and its pseudo-realism. At the same time, they are profoundly related to the human mind, that is to say, to the subject, which is itself immersed in culture, society, and history. The concept of system demands a natural science that is at the same time a human science.

Phantom Concept and Pilot Concept

In its dual nature, the system is a phantom-concept. Like the phantom, it takes on the form of material beings; but like the phantom, it is immaterial. The system links idealism and realism, without letting itself be trapped by one or the other. It is neither "form," nor "content," nor elements conceived in isolation, nor the whole by itself, but all of these linked in and through the organization that transforms them. The system is a model that lets itself be modeled by the qualities proper to phenomenality. The idea of organization is a logical simulation, but as it comprises alogical elements (antagonisms, emergents), it is equally the reflection of what it simulates and by what it stimulates it. This is to say, the concept of system is no magic formula or some vehicle that might transport us to the state of knowledge. It offers us no security. It must be straddled, corrected, and guided. It is a pilot-concept, but only on condition that it is piloted.

The Subject/Object Transaction

The concept of system can only be constructed in and through the subject/object transaction, and not through the elimination of one term by the other.

Naïve realism, which takes the system to be a real object, eliminates the problem of the subject; naïve nominalism, which takes the system to be an ideal schema, eliminates the object. However, it also eliminates the problem of the subject, for it considers in the ideal model, not its subjective structure, but its degree of manipulative and predictive efficiency.

In fact, however, the object, whether real or ideal, is also an object that depends upon a *subject*.

Through this systemic route, the observer—excluded from classical science—and the subject—excoriated and rejected as so much metaphysical trash—make their reentry into the very heart of *physis*. This brings us to a key idea: there is no longer a *physis* isolated from humanity, which can be isolated from its understanding, its logic, its culture, and its society. There are no objects independent of a subject.

So understood, therefore, the notion of system leads the subject not only to verify its observation, but to integrate the same within the process of self-observation.

Observing and Observed System

Thus the observation and study of a system must link to one another, in systemic terms. Physical organization and the organization of ideas. The observed system—and consequently the organized physis of which it is a part—and the observer-system, along with the anthroposocial organization of which it is a part, become interrelated in a crucial way: the observer is as much a part of the definition of observed system as the observed system is a part of the intellect and culture of the observer. By and through such an interrelation, a new systemic totality is created, which becomes the meta-system with respect to both and it admits the possibility of finding a point of view that permits the observation of the set constituted by the observer and his or her observation. The systemic relation between the observer and observation can be conceived in a complex manner whereby the mind of the observer/conceptualizer, his or her theory, and more widely, his or her culture and society, are considered as so many ecosystemic envelopes of the physical system being studied. The mental/cultural creates the system under consideration, yet it coproduces it and nourishes its relative autonomy. This is the view that I provisionally adopt here.

We can, and indeed must, go further in the search for a meta-systemic point of view: we can no longer escape the key epistemological problem involved in the relation between, on one hand, the polysystemic group constituted by the subject-conceptualizer and his or her anthropo-social rootedness, and on the other, the polysystemic group constituted by the object-system and its physical rootedness. This would involve the elaboration of a meta-system of reference as the locus for the intercommunication and interorganization of both groups. It is from this perspective—both denied and forbidden by classical science—that a path is cleared for new theoretical and epistemological development. Such development requires not only that the observer observe him or herself observing systems, but also that he or she make the effort to know his or her knowing.

Finally, the systemic articulation established between the anthroposocial and the physical universe, via the concept of system, suggests that the characteristic of organization is fundamental to all systems. The possibility of articulating, in systemic terms, the organization of physis as well as the organization of knowledge, implies an initial organizational homology. This homology would permit the organizational retroaction (feedback) of our anthropo-social understanding on the physical world out of which this understanding has emerged through the process of evolution. Here I wish merely to stress that the theory of organization will be of increasing concern to the organization of theory. The concept of system lends itself to theoretical elaborations that allow itself to be outstripped. The complex theory of the system, in other words, transforms the theoretical system that forms it.

I hope this much is clear: It is not a question here of a Hegelian ambition to dominate the world of systems with the System of Ideas. It is a question of an inquiry into the relation, both hidden and extraordinary, between the organization of knowledge and the knowledge of organization.

REFERENCES

Ashby, W.R. (1956). *An introduction to cybernetics*. London: Chapman and Hall.

Atlan, H. (1972). *L'Organisation biologique et le theorie de l'information*. Paris: Herman.

Beer, S. (1960). Below the twilight arch. *General Systems Yearbook*, p. 16.

de Rosnay, J. (1975). *Le macroscope*. (The macroscope.) Paris: Seuil.

Guenther, G. (1962). Cybernetical ontology and transjunctional operations, in *Self-organizing systems*. Washington: Spartan Books.

Morin, E. (1977). *La methode 1* [Method, 1]. Paris: Seuil.

Needham, J. (1977). *La science chinoise et l'Occident* [Chinese science and the west.]. Paris: Seuil.

Maruyama, M. (1974). Paradigmatology and its applications to cross-disciplinary, cross-professional and cross-cultural-communications. *Dialectica, 28*, 135-196.

Spencer-Brown, J. (1969). *The laws of form*. London: Allen & Unwin.

von Foerster, H. (1983). *Observing systems*. Seaside, CA: Intersystems Publications.

APPENDIX 2

A NEW SCIENCE
OF AUTONOMY

Translated by Sean M. Kelly

Traditional scientific understanding can only recognize determinism in the universe. Every social science founded on this model of understanding can only gloss over the ideas of freedom and autonomy, of subject and agent, in whatever form. The ideas of freedom, autonomy, subject, and agent, according to this model, arise from mere subjective and intersubjective experience, which science justly eliminates.

There is, therefore, an irremediable alternative between, on the one hand, a science that abolishes in its very vision the fundamental characteristics of human reality, and on the other, consciousness and an ethic of freedom that can find only a metaphysical foundation.

In fact, however, a scientific revolution began in the last half-century which, starting from the very heart of *physis*, has made possible the elaboration of new science of autonomy. I can only summarize and catalogue the basic principles *scienza nuova* (I devote most of *La Methode* to these problems).

1. The science of autonomy is founded on the new vision of the physical universe. This universe is no longer subject solely to deterministic order, but obeys the rules of the game of order/disorder/organization. For the last hundred years, in all sectors, physics recognizes chance and works with chance. Henceforth we see the universe in terms of probability and improbability, and we have discovered that it is in the zones of improbability that innovations, the pilot-fish of becoming, can arise. In fact, therefore, our physical, biological, and anthropo-social universe, the universe of our existence and understanding, is a mix/combination of order (laws, regularities, constants structures, probabilities) and disorder (chance, agitations, random meetings, collisions, dispersions). This apparent incoherent universe is nevertheless the only one where we can conceive of becoming and innovation. We cannot see how change and the new could arise in a totally deterministic universe; we cannot see organization in a totally random universe.

2. The science of autonomy emerged in the physical sphere itself, via cybernetics and systems theory (which are partial versions) as the science of organization. Organization is the arrangement of relations among components or individuals that produce a complex organized unity, or system, endowed with a relative autonomy. Organization constitutes and maintains autonomous systems, that is, the autonomy of these systems.

3. The systemic idea of emergence and the cybernetic idea of retroaction (feedback) are two fundamental ideas of complex thinking that allow for the conception of systemic/organizational autonomy. Emergents are the new qualities/properties (in relation to the constitutive properties/qualities taken in isolation), including the prop-

erties/qualities of autonomy emanating from organization. Emergents feed back on the conditions and instruments of their formation, and, in the process, maintain the perenniality of system (Morin, 1977). Retroaction (feedback) is the return of an effect on the conditions that produced it. Thus, atoms, molecules, suns and, of course, living beings, are organization/systems disposing of emergent qualities that are nonexistent at the level of the constitutive parts conceived in isolation. The single cell for example, disposes of qualities of life that are nonexistent in each of the macromolecules of protein and DNA, as well as in the cytoplasm or the nucleus when isolated from one another.

4. The physical universe presents to us active organizations, which have this remarkable characteristic of self-producing and self-organizing themselves without breaking the continuity of their proper autonomy and existence. The property of self-organization-is is recursive, which is to say that it causes/produces the effects/products necessary for its own regeneration. A living organization is a self-organization that produces and reproduces itself according to an informational heritage inscribed in the genes.

5. Self-production produces being and existence as it produces the constituents necessary for this being and existence. In other words, the complex notion of self-organization permits us to conceive of beings that are relatively autonomous as beings while remaining subject to the necessities and hazards of *existence*.

6. Self-organizing beings—which, on our planet, are essentially living beings—are systems that are not only *closed* (protecting their integrity and their identity) but also *open* to their environment, from which they derive matter, energy, information, and organization. Self-organizing beings, therefore, are *self-eco-organizing beings*, which leads to this fundamental complex idea: *all autonomy constitutes itself in and through ecological dependence*. As far as we are concerned, our ecological independence is not only natural but social and culture as well.

7. Living beings are machine-beings whose self-eco-organization operates through the computation/communication of information. Computation comprises calculation and logical operations that allow for decision. Every cellular being, on the basis of its genetic information and the information that it extracts from its environment, computes for its life, its survival, and its reproduction. It computes in an auto-referential and egocentric manner. This is what I call the *computo*, or computation in the first person, which establishes at each instant the autonomy of an individual subject (the notion of subject being defined here by self-reference and the

occupation of the ego-centric site by a *computo*). We thus have a biological basis for the no notion of the autonomous individual, which, in its very autonomy, depends not only on its environment, but also on its genetic heritage.

8. The higher animals dispose of a neuro-cerebral apparatus of increasing complexity and performance that elaborates strategies (of knowing and acting) and which, apprehending or producing situations demanding choice, makes decisions. It is on this foundation that the possibility of freedom developed in human beings. This freedom does not drop from heaven, but emerges from the most complex self-organization there is: anthropo-social self-organization.

Thus, it is not the mixture of determinism and chance that produces freedom—there must be the possibility of decision and choice. There must, therefore, be a self-eco-organizing being capable of computing and cogitating the situations that confront it, capable of deciding between scenarios and commanding the chosen action This freedom implies a double determination: the internal organizational determination and the determination of external events; it also implies a relative internal indeterminacy (the possibility of choice) and the presence of chance and hazard in the external environment (which allows for the insertion of free action).

Free action depends upon the knowledge and utilization of determinations (constants, structures, laws). At the same time, free action depends upon the chance possibilities that present themselves in the situation in which it intervenes (strategy).

Freedom is an emergent, it emerges within the given internal and external conditions proper to an self-eco-organization. Freedom, in this sense, is slave to these conditions of emergence. It is totally dependent upon self-organization, which, in turn, depends upon external ecological conditions (if only to nourish itself, to self-reorganize and self-repair itself). The autonomy of individuals is acquired through innumerable dependencies: one must be nourished and loved by the parents, must learn to speak and to write, must go to school, university, and encode a highly diversified culture to acquire ever greater possibilities of autonomy. Autonomy, therefore, should always be conceived not in opposition to, but in complementarity with, the idea of dependence.

But once it has emerged, autonomy retroacts (feeds back) on its formative conditions, retroacts on the organization that produced it, and in developing the autonomy of this very organization, becomes increasingly suited to the operation of free acts.

In this manner, freedom and determinism cease being substantial notions: they become, instead, complex notions that in order to be thought, require a principle of physical complexity (the relation order/disorder/organization), a principle of organizational complexity including the notions of emergence, retroaction, and a principle of autonomy/dependence.

We now have the conceptual tools to think together, in association and interaction—no longer in mutual exclusion; we have determinism and freedom. An act can be at once determined and free. It can be more or less free. We are more or less free according to our inner aptitudes for organizing our freedom, as well as according to the economic, social, political, and historical determinations that enclose, enslave, or, on the contrary, open up possibilities of autonomy.

We can now conceive of the complex reality of our relation to life, biology, society, and history: we possess genes that possess us; we live our life as a destiny, while we mould it into experience; we make the society that makes us; we make the history that makes us . . .

We must cease looking upon economic and social life either as the product of pure determinism (each ideology favoring its decisive determinant) or as a theater for confrontation of free wills. Each vision, in fact, is impossible. The philosophies of free will recognize, from below, the presence of objective determinants in the socio-political sphere, and must ceaselessly take into account constraints that reduce the scope of the will. All determinist ideology, on its side, recognizes voluntary action, but without being able to justify it theoretically. Marxism, for example, is a two-level ideology. On the first level, it is a deterministic theory that predicts the necessary collapse of bourgeois society and the advent of socialism; on the second level, it is an ethic of revolt and emancipation. The whole ethic of the party is founded upon conscious realization and voluntary action; Lenin accorded a key role to strategy and decision that, at the propitious moment, could upset the course of history. Nevertheless, the two levels do not coincide; the will has no place in the theory and intervenes but clandestinely.

Today, it is more necessary than ever, and it is at last possible, to formulate a scientific conception that allows for the comprehension of the complex relation between autonomy/dependence and freedom/determinism, terms that, although they become complementary, remain concurrent and antagonistic. Henceforth, we have at our disposal the paradigmatic, theoretical, and conceptual foundations for the notions of autonomy, self-organization, without which the anthropo-social sciences would be illusions, pure and simple, without which political theory would become, in its very principle, manipulative and enslaving.

NOTES

1. E. Morin, *La méthode*, volumes 1 and 2, Paris, Le Seuil, 1977-1980. New edition, "Points" Collection, Le Seuil, 1981-1985.

2. E. Morin, *Science avec conscience*, Paris, Fayard, 1982. New edition, "Points" collection, Le Seuil, 1990, p. 304-9.

3. Ibid., p. 24

4. Cf. J.-L. Le Moigne, *La théorie du système général*, PUF, 1990 edition; cf. Also the special issue of the *Revue internationale de systémique*, 2, 90, "Systémique de la complexité," presented by J.-L. Le Moigne.

5. M. Maruyama, Paradigmatology, and its applications to cross-disciplinary. Cross-professional and cross-cultural communication, *Cybernetika*, 17, 1974, p. 136-156, 27-51.

6. Since this text written in 1976, there have been remarkable works with a focus on complexity, notably by Jean-Louis Le Moigne in *La théorie du systeme général*, PUF, new edition 1990, the work by Yves Barel, *Le paradoxe et le système*, PUG, 1979, and *Le concept de système politique* by Jean-Louis Vuillerme, PUF, 1989.)

7. This has however been useful in its spectacular aspect: the systemic study of the Meadows report on growth (MIT) introduced the idea that the planet Earth is a system open to the biosphere, and elicited fruitful consciousness raising and alarm. But, of course, the choice of parameters and variables were arbitrary, and it is in the pseudo-exactitude of the calculations, in the "technocratic" simplification that the bad side of the triumphant systemism resides.

8. J. Piaget, *Biologie et connaissance,* Paris, Gallimard, 1967

9. J. Schangler, *Les métaphores de l'organism*, Paris, Vrin, 1971, p.35.

10. J. von Neumann, *Theory of Self-Reproducing Automata*, 1966, University of Illinois Press, Urbana.

11. The singular idea was to isolate variables in permanent interaction in a system, but never to consider precisely the permanent interactions of the system. Also, paradoxically, naïve studies, close to phenomena, were much more complex, which is to say, in the end, more "scientific" than the pretentious quantitative studies on statistical bulldozers, guided by drivers with small brains. And so it is, I say immodestly, that my studies of phenomena, attempted to seize the complexity of a multi-dimensional social change in a community in Bretagne, or in the midst of the action and the burgeoning of the events of May 1968. The only method I had was to attempt to shed light on the multiple aspects of phenomena, and to attempt to seize moving relationships. Connect, always connect. What a much richer method, even at a theoretical level, than blind theories, epistemologically and logically armed, methodologically apt to confront any challenge, except, obviously, the complexity of reality.

12. Cf. Abraham A. Moles, *Les Sciences de l'imprecis*, Le Seuil, 1990.

13. G. Gunther, "Cybernetical Ontology and transjunctionnal Operations" in Yovitz, Jacobi, Goldstein eds., *Self-organizing Systems*, Washington: Spartan Books.

14. G. Gunther, op. cit., p. 383.

15. Ibid., p. 351.

16. Ibid.

17. E. Schrödinger, *Mind and Matter,* Cambridge University Press, 1959, p. 52.

18. Ibid., p. 64.

19. N. Bohr, *Lumières et vie*, Congrès international de thérapie par la lumière, 1932.

20. "But we must at the same time break the objective/metaphysical frame where chance was Absurd, to pass into the level of relation between the observer and the observation, the subject and the object, the system and the ecosystem, where we will always meet chance, in other words, a gap in determination and prediction." E. Morin, "L'événement sphinx," *Communication: L'Evénement*, 18, 1972.
21. J. Jaynes, *The Origins of Consciousness in the Breakdown of the Bicameral Mind.* Boston: Houghton Mifflin, 1976.
22. L. Wittgenstein, "Remarques sul le Rameau d'or de Frazer," *Actes de la recherche en science socials*, 16 sept 1977, p. 35-42.
23. Based on "La complexité est un noeud gordien," in *Management France*, Feb–Mar 1987, p. 4–8.
24. From "La complexité, grille de lecture des organisations" in *Management France*, January.February 1986, pp. 6–8, and "Complexité et organisation" in *La production des connaissance scientifiques de l'administration*, The generation of scientific administrative knowledge, under the direction of Michel Audet et Jean-Louis Maloin, Presses de l'Université Laval, Québec, 1986, p. 135-154.

AUTHOR INDEX

SUBJECT INDEX